60

THE WORLD'S 60 BEST ROAST DISHES...
PERIOD.
VÉRONIQUE PARADIS

PHOTOGRAPHER: Antoine Sicotte
ART DIRECTORS: Antoine Sicotte & Véronique Paradis
GRAPHIC DESIGNER: Laurie Auger
COVER DESIGNER: Laurie Auger
FOOD STYLIST: Véronique Paradis
ENGLISH TRANSLATOR: Lorien Jones
COPY EDITOR: Anna Phelan

PROJECT EDITOR: Antoine Ross Trempe

ISBN: 978-2-924155-10-3

Legal Deposit: 2013
Bibliothèque et Archives du Québec
Library and Archives Canada
ISBN: 978-2-924155-10-3

The publisher acknowledges the financial support of the Government of Canada through the Canada Book Fund (CBF) for its publishing activities and the support of the Government of Quebec through the tax credits for book publishing program (SODEC).

Originally published under the title
"Les 60 meilleurs plats rôtis du monde... Point final."

PRINTED IN CANADA

Discover our upcoming books and much more!
WWW.FACEBOOK.COM/THEWORLDS60BEST

THE WORLD'S 60 BEST

ROAST DISHES

PERIOD.

THE WORLD'S 60 BEST

ROAST DISHES

PERIOD.

ABOUT THIS BOOK

The 60 roast dishes in this book are, *in our opinion*, the 60 best roast dishes in the world. Our team of chefs, writers, and foodies explored everything the culinary world has to offer to create this collection of the world's 60 best roast dishes.

We based our recipes on the following criteria:

QUALITY OF INGREDIENTS
ORIGINALITY
TASTE
APPEARANCE
SIMPLICITY

Are these our personal favorite roast dishes? Of course! But rest assured, our team of passionate, dedicated gourmets put time and loving care into formulating and testing each recipe in order to provide you with the 60 best roast dishes ever. In fact, our chef brought each freshly made dish straight from the kitchen into the studio—no colorants, no sprays, no special effects added—and after each photo shoot, our creative team happily devoured the very roast dishes you see in these photos.

We hope you'll enjoy discovering these recipes and using this book as much as we enjoyed making it.

TABLE OF CONTENTS

CREDITS 002

ABOUT THIS BOOK 009

INTRO 017

FLAVOR & COST LEGEND 018

A SHORT HISTORY OF ROAST DISHES 021

MUST-HAVE TOOLS 023

TIPS & TRICKS 025

HOW-TO GUIDE 027

GLOSSARY 029

THE CHEF'S SECRET 031

RACK OF PORK WITH BARBECUE GLAZE	032
THE HOLIDAY TURKEY	034
LAMB WITH WINE & GRAPEVINE LEAVES	036
WINTER DELIGHT	038
ANCHO ESPRESSO BEEF	040
PORK ORLOFF	044
CORNISH HEN WITH GRAPES	046
ROASTED MARROW ON TOAST	048
PORK & ROASTED PEACHES	050
LAMB SHAWARMA	052
SWEET & NUTTY BRUSSELS SPROUTS	056
BLUE CHEESE & APPLE PORK WELLINGTON	058
CLASSIC MEAT LOAF	060
SALT-CRUSTED SALMON & ASPARAGUS	062
PIRI-PIRI CHICKEN	064
SUNDAY SAUSAGE ROAST	068
TURKEY & CRANBERRY ROLL-UP	070
VEAL PROVENÇAL	072
PORTOBELLO PORK ROAST	074
RUSSIAN ROAST BEEF	076
ROASTED RED PEPPERS	080
PEKING DUCK	082
CITRUSY BARBECUE SALMON	084
JERK CHICKEN	086
PORK BELLY WITH MAPLE CALVADOS GLAZE	088
LEMONY CHICKEN & WILD MUSHROOMS	092
BEST-EVER HONEY-GLAZED HAM	094
SUMMER VEGGIES	096
KARATE QUAIL!	098
RUSTIC ROAST BEEF SANDWICH	100
ROASTED GARLIC BUTTER	104
TROUT WITH SUNNY SALSA	106
THE ORIGINAL ROASTED CHICKEN	108
PULLED PORK	110
FILET MIGNON & BÉARNAISE SAUCE	112
ROASTED CARROTS	116
WORLD-FAMOUS BARBECUE CHICKEN	118
RIBS WITH BOURBON BARBECUE SAUCE	120
RACK OF LAMB & PERSILLADE	122
MONKFISH, TAPENADE & PROSCIUTTO	124
ROASTED SQUASH & HUMMUS	128
FOUR ALARM CHICKEN WINGS	130
TRADITIONAL ROAST BEEF	132
BACON-WRAPPED RABBIT	134
COD WITH CLAM SAUCE	136
ROASTED POTATOES	140
PORK ROAST & MELT-IN-YOUR-MOUTH POTATOES	142
BEEF & RED WINE MARINADE	144
LEMON & OLIVE LAMB	146
SWEET POTATOES, APPLES & PECANS	148
TANDOORI CHICKEN DRUMSTICKS	152
HASSELBACK POTATOES	154
GUINEA FOWL WITH LENTILS & LARDONS	156
RED SNAPPER, TOMATOES & FENNEL	158
VEAL, SUNDRIED TOMATOES & GOAT CHEESE	160
RACK OF LAMB WITH POMEGRANATE SAUCE	164
CRISPY PESTO CHICKEN LEGS	166
RISING SUN RIBS	168
ROASTED CAULIFLOWER	170
BEER & MAPLE LAMB	172
INGREDIENTS INDEX	176
MARINADES, GLAZES, SAUCES, SEASONINGS, ETC.	180

INTRO

Every one of the 60 best roast dishes in this book features a flavor and cost legend (see pages 018 and 019) to guide your taste buds as well as your wallet in choosing the perfect dish. You will also find a glossary of culinary terms (page 029), handy cooking tips and tricks (page 025), and a list of must-have kitchen tools (page 023) that will help you create the world's BEST roast dishes. Finally, use the easy-to-follow table of contents (pages 010 and 011) and ingredients index (pages 176 to 179) to find everything you're looking for.

Impress guests with your food knowledge from our informative "Did you know?" sidebars, and take your meals to the next level thanks to our tasty tips and serving suggestions!

Bon appétit!

SPICY

RICH

COST

LEGEND

HOT • PEPPERY • ZESTY

 LOW MEDIUM  HIGH

CREAMY • BUTTERY • LUSCIOUS

 LOW MEDIUM HIGH

COST OF INGREDIENTS

 LOW MEDIUM HIGH

A SHORT HISTORY OF ROAST DISHES

Upon hearing the word "roast," the first thing that typically comes to mind is, of course, meat! By classic definition, roasting is the technique of cooking meat, poultry, game, or fish by exposing it to the direct, dry heat of a flame or grill, or to the radiant, dry heat of an oven, which browns the surface of the food and makes it tender and tantalizingly tasty. But as everyone knows, meat isn't the only food that can be roasted. Roasting coaxes the sweetness from earthy root and bulb vegetables, takes the bite out of garlic and transforms it into a soft, spreadable condiment, and with just a bit of oil, salt, and pepper intensifies the flavors of cauliflower, bell peppers, and tomatoes.

Humans have actually been roasting food for thousands of years. Roasting began as an open-air activity, with meat on a spit turned over an open fire. Scientists have even discovered that Neanderthals, an extinct sub-species of humans long viewed as meat eaters, roasted vegetables and medicinal plants. Many different cultures roast cereals and plants to add flavor and provide sustenance during times of hardship: in Indian, Pakistani, and Bangladeshi cuisines, for example, chickpea flour is roasted to make it less bitter, and in the isolated mountain regions of Tuscany, where food is often scarce during the winter months, roasted chestnuts have long been used to make flour for polenta, pasta, pancakes, and desserts.

The roasting process is also what produces the characteristic flavor of coffee beans, and is a necessary step in chocolate production: it kills any bacteria or mold on the cocoa beans, removes bitterness, and develops that distinctive chocolaty taste and smell.

While most North Americans and Europeans are more familiar with roasting food in a classic oven, spit-roasting is still very common in many regions of the world. Méchoui is an iconic North African dish of whole sheep or lamb spit-roasted horizontally on a barbecue and served as an appetizer on special occasions. Traditionally, the host will offer pieces of grilled meat to the event's most distinguished guests; utensils are never used for this dish, as the meat should be so tender at the end of cooking that the meat literally falls off the bone and pulls apart easily. Döner kebab, which means "roasting spit" in Turkish, is made by roasting meat on a vertical spit. This popular street food originated in Bursa, Turkey, in the 19th century, and can be made with lamb, beef, or chicken. The seasoned meat is layered on the spit in the shape of an inverted cone and turned slowly in front of a vertical rotisserie, and then sliced into very thin shavings and wrapped in a flatbread with vegetables and sauce.

The World's 60 Best Roast Dishes offers a diverse selection of main and side dishes for every occasion, with your favorite classics and bold new flavor combinations. So fire up the oven and get roasting!

MUST-HAVE TOOLS

FOR THE WORLD'S BEST ROAST DISHES

1. A **chef's knife** for chopping, cubing, dicing, slicing, and mincing

2. A quality **pair of stainless steel tongs** for flipping meat, poultry, seafood, and vegetables

3. A **food processor** for chopping and puréeing ingredients

4. A **peeler** for peeling vegetables

5. A **mortar** and **pestle** for crushing, grinding, and mixing spices to give your roasts the freshest flavor

6. A **ladle** for basting roasts during cooking

7. A **small pot** for reducing sauces

8. A **basting brush** for brushing on delicious glazes

9. **Aluminum foil** for covering roasts when in the oven or when resting after cooking

10. **Parchment paper** for covering baking sheets and preventing food from sticking

11. A **roasting pan** for making the world's 60 best roasts

12. A **large baking sheet** for beautifully roasted, golden brown vegetables

13. **Oven mitts** for safely removing roasts from the oven

14. A **meat thermometer** for checking the internal temperature of your roasts and making sure they're perfectly cooked

15. A **carving fork** for easy slicing

16. A **grill rack** for elevating your roasts and allowing them to cook evenly

TIPS & TRICKS

FOR CREATING THE WORLD'S BEST ROAST DISHES

1. Your local or supermarket butcher and fishmonger are your greatest allies in the quest to find the perfect cut of meat. If you're having trouble finding the right cut, just ask! And always check to make sure the meat is fresh.

2. Bring red meat (but never poultry) to room temperature before roasting. Taking a piece of meat out of the refrigerator ten to fifteen minutes before cooking, depending on the size, will allow it to cook more evenly, avoiding an overdone exterior and red, raw interior. To prevent bacteria from forming, however, it's best not to leave it out too long.

3. Timing is key when it comes to roasting. Put a note on the piece of meat to remind you when to add the marinade, take it out of the fridge, and preheat the oven, especially if you're cooking for guests!

4. Because every oven and every cut of meat is different, it's a good idea to purchase a meat thermometer. And there's no need to buy a complicated-to-use, ultra-modern model; a classic thermometer is just as accurate and will do the job just as well.

5. Regular basting is essential if you want a roast that's juicy on the inside and golden brown on the outside. It takes a bit more effort, but it's worth it!

6. Avoid cutting into your roast to check for doneness. This allows the precious juices to escape, resulting in a drier piece of meat. Use a meat thermometer instead, as it will only leave a small hole.

7. Certain poultry parts, like the wings, roast more quickly than others, and tend to burn while the breast is still cooking. For an evenly cooked bird, just cover the parts that have finished cooking with aluminum foil; the meatier parts will crisp up to a beautiful golden brown, and you'll end up with a roast bird fit for a king!

8. Remember to let red meat rest after cooking, before slicing and serving. Resting allows the juices to settle and redistribute back through the meat, and the meat to continue to cook slightly longer. If you slice your roast right after removing it from the oven, that tasty liquid will pool out and the meat will be dry.

9. Whether you're using store-bought or homemade sauce, always save the drippings that collect at the bottom of the pan. This liquid is packed with concentrated flavor and will add flavor to future dishes.

10. Roast leftovers don't have to be boring. Use them to stuff sandwiches or paninis, grill them up for fajita filling, sauté them in a stir-fry, or toss with pasta and sauce. Delicious meals in minutes!

HOW-TO GUIDE

COOKING MEAT AND POULTRY TO PERFECTION

Every oven has its own personality: some models are more powerful than others, and some have more precise temperature control. Because of this, a meat thermometer is the best way to tell if your roasts are ready and cooked to perfection. Digital meat thermometers are accurate and widely available, but the standard dial models work just as well.

To properly measure the internal temperature of a piece of meat, just insert the thermometer into the center and wait until the temperature stops climbing. Make sure the thermometer probe isn't touching bone—you'll end up with a false reading.

When measuring the internal temperature of poultry, it's very important to check the breasts and the legs, since their cooking time is slightly different.

Never test temperature in the same spot: heat will enter into the hole made by the thermometer and will result in a false reading.

TYPE OF MEAT	INTERNAL TEMPERATURE IN FAHRENHEIT (CELSIUS), BEFORE RESTING		
	SLIGHTLY PINK	MEDIUM	DONE
1. CHICKEN	-	-	176°F (80°C)
2. TURKEY	-	-	176°F (80°C)
3. PORK	-	136°F (58°C)	150°F (65°C)
4. VEAL	-	130°F (55°C)	140°F (60°C)
5. BEEF AND LAMB	122°F (50°C)	130°F (55°C)	140°F (60°C)

GLOSSARY

1. SEASON

To improve the flavor of a dish by adding salt and pepper to taste.

2. BLANCH

To cook vegetables briefly in boiling salted water.

3. DICE

A basic knife cut in which food is cut into cubes.

4. DEGLAZE

To remove and dissolve caramelized bits of food at the bottom of a pan in order to make a jus or a sauce.

5. THINLY SLICE

To cut into thin, equal slices.

6. REDUCE

To thicken a liquid by evaporating over heat.

7. SEAR

To cook in fat (butter or oil) at a high temperature to obtain a golden or brown crust.

8. ZEST

To remove the zest (outer skin) of citrus fruits with a zester, grater, or peeling knife.

9. SAUTÉ

To cook, stirring, over high heat in a pan, Dutch oven, or heavy-bottomed pot.

10. WILT

To cook certain vegetables (spinach, Swiss chard, kale, sorrel, etc.) over low heat, with or without a fat, in order to reduce their volume and release some of their liquid.

11. BRUSH

To coat food with a thin layer of liquid or sauce using a brush or the back of a spoon.

12. CHOP

To cut into small pieces with a sharp instrument (knife or food processor).

THE CHEF'S SECRET

Every seasoned chef will attest that the real secret to creating a successful dish is to *taste! taste! taste!* Taste before and after seasoning, add some heat or a squeeze of lemon juice if you think your dish needs a little kick, or go ahead and double the herbs or even the cheese! The most important thing is to follow your instincts and your senses. Listen for that telltale sizzle, inhale the tantalizing aromas, and CONSTANTLY taste your food so you can get to know your dish in all its stages.

There you have it—the simple secret to creating delicious, original dishes.

1

RACK OF PORK WITH BARBECUE GLAZE

SERVES 4

FOR BARBECUE GLAZE

1/4 cup (60 ml) store-bought chili sauce
2 tbsp cider vinegar
1/4 cup (60 ml) brown sugar
3 cloves garlic, chopped
2 tbsp soy sauce

FOR PORK

2 tbsp vegetable oil
1 whole rack of pork (4 chops)
Salt and freshly ground pepper

FOR GARNISH

12 new potatoes, halved
8 sprigs fresh thyme
2 tomatoes, diced
1 onion, thinly sliced
1/2 cup (125 ml) white wine
1 cup (250 ml) chorizo sausage, cut into 1/2-inch cubes

PREPARATION

In a small bowl, combine all glaze ingredients.

In a pan, heat vegetable oil over high heat. Season rack of pork with salt and pepper and sear on all sides. Brush meat with glaze.

Place potatoes, thyme, tomatoes, onion, wine, and chorizo in a large baking dish, mix well, and push towards the outer edges of the baking dish to create a space in the center for the pork. Place pork in the center, with the meatiest side facing up.

Roast in a 400°F (200°C) oven for 40 minutes, brushing with glaze every 10 minutes. Remove from oven and let sit for 8 to 10 minutes. Slice into 4 chops and serve with potatoes and chorizo mixture on the side.

THE HOLIDAY TURKEY

SERVES 10

DID YOU KNOW?

Cooked, peeled chestnuts can be found at most fine grocery stores, but you can also roast your own! Here's how: With a knife, cut an X into the side of each chestnut. Arrange on a baking sheet and roast in a 425°F (220°C) oven for 30 minutes. Remove from oven and let cool. Once they are cool enough to handle, take a cloth and rub the chestnuts to remove the skin. Enjoy!

Marinating time: 12 hours
Prep time: 40 minutes
Cook time: 3 hours

1 whole turkey (about 9 lbs)
Water

FOR TURKEY BRINE

8 cups water
1 cup (250 ml) coarse salt
3/4 cup (180 ml) sugar
2 tbsp mild paprika
2 tbsp whole peppercorns
4 sprigs fresh thyme
2 bay leaves
5 cloves garlic, crushed
24 ice cubes

FOR STUFFING

1 tbsp butter
4 cloves garlic, chopped
10 button mushrooms, chopped
20 cooked, peeled chestnuts, roughly chopped
(see "Did you know?" sidebar)
2 tbsp fresh rosemary, chopped
2 cups (500 ml) sausage meat
1/4 baguette, cut into 1-inch cubes
2 eggs
1/3 cup (80 ml) 35% cream

PREPARATION

For turkey brine: Combine all brine ingredients, except ice cubes, in a large pot. Bring to a boil, reduce heat to low, and let simmer for 5 minutes. After 5 minutes, remove from heat, add ice cubes, and mix well. If brine is still warm, refrigerate until cool. Put turkey into brine, making sure it's completely covered. Refrigerate for at least 12 hours.

For stuffing: In a pan, heat butter and sauté garlic and mushrooms for 5 to 6 minutes. Remove from heat and let cool. In a large bowl, combine mushrooms and garlic with remaining stuffing ingredients. Mix well.

Stuff turkey cavity and then rub skin with 2 tbsp vegetable oil. Truss turkey with kitchen string and place on a grill rack in a roasting pan. Pour 1 inch of water into the bottom of the pan and cook in a 350°F (175°C) oven for 3 hours, basting turkey with its cooking juices every 30 minutes. Slice and serve.

LAMB WITH WINE & GRAPEVINE LEAVES

SERVES 4

DID YOU KNOW?

After the Renaissance, many paintings and sculptures depicting nudity were judged to be indecent. Vine leaves were added to many classic works of art, to cover the "offensive" parts.

Marinating time: 4 to 12 hours
Prep time: 30 minutes
Cook time: 3 hours

FOR LAMB

1 boneless shoulder of lamb
12 store-bought grapevine leaves, from a jar

FOR WHITE WINE MARINADE

4 cloves garlic, chopped
1/4 cup (60 ml) fresh mint, chopped
1/4 cup (60 ml) fresh oregano, chopped
Juice of 1 lemon
1/2 cup (125 ml) white wine
1/4 cup (60 ml) olive oil
Salt and freshly ground pepper

PREPARATION

In a small bowl, combine all white wine marinade ingredients. Place lamb shoulder in a large dish and completely cover with marinade. Cover and refrigerate for at least 4 hours.

With a small knife, remove the thickest parts of the grapevine leaf stems.

Place a large piece of aluminum foil vertically on a flat work surface, the narrowest part facing you. Lightly oil the foil and lay out 6 grapevine leaves to form a large square, and then top with another layer of 6 leaves.

Remove meat from marinade and roll it up into a log. Place on top of grapevine leaves and use the foil as a guide to roll it up as tightly as possible in the leaves. Tie with kitchen string, making sure the grapevine leaves are securely wrapped around the meat. Wrap entire roast in the aluminum foil.

Place wrapped roast in a roasting pan and pour 1 inch of water into the bottom of the pan. Cover and cook in a 350°F (175°C) oven for 3 hours.

After 3 hours, remove from oven and unwrap and untie roast. Serve with cooking juices as a gravy.

4

WINTER DELIGHT

SERVES 6

Prep time: 20 minutes
Cook time: 1 hour

INGREDIENTS

1 turnip, peeled and cut into 1-inch cubes
2 carrots, peeled and cut into 1-inch rounds
1 white potato, washed and cut into 1-inch cubes
1 sweet potato, peeled and cut into 1-inch cubes
1 onion, cut into 1/2-inch strips
2 cloves garlic, thinly sliced
6 sprigs fresh thyme
1 sprig rosemary, leaves removed
1/3 cup (80 ml) olive oil
Salt and freshly ground pepper

PREPARATION

In a large bowl, combine all ingredients. Season mixture with salt and pepper and spread evenly on a baking sheet. Cook in a 375°F (190°C) oven, on the center rack, for 1 hour. Serve as a side dish with one of the world's 60 best roasts!

 **TASTY TIP**

Instead of reheating your leftover roasted vegetables, toss them with a few simple ingredients to transform them into a flavorpacked salad! Just combine 2 cups (500 ml) roasted vegetables in a bowl with 2 tbsp mayonnaise and 1 tbsp sherry vinegar. For a hearty, nutritious salad, add cubed ham, quartered hard-boiled eggs, and a bit of wholegrain mustard. Great for a quick dinner or for packed lunches!

5

ANCHO ESPRESSO BEEF

SERVES 8

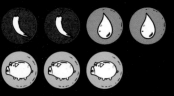

TASTY TIP

Serve with a complementing side dish of mushrooms and onions sautéed with a bit of balsamic vinegar.

DID YOU KNOW?

The ancho chili is actually a dried poblano pepper.

Marinating time: 2 hours
Prep time: 15 minutes
Cook time: 1 hour and 30 minutes

FOR ANCHO ESPRESSO SEASONING

1/4 cup (60 ml) brown sugar
2 tbsp ancho chili powder
2 tbsp finely ground espresso coffee
1 tsp garlic powder
1 tsp onion powder
1 tsp salt
1/4 tsp ground coriander
1 tsp freshly ground pepper

FOR RIB ROAST

1 prime rib roast (about 4-1/2 lbs)
2 tbsp vegetable oil
1/2 cup (125 ml) red wine
1/2 cup (125 ml) water

PREPARATION

In a bowl, combine all ancho espresso seasoning ingredients. Rub entire surface of meat with this mixture.

Transfer to a dish, cover, and refrigerate for 2 hours. Let meat sit at room temperature for 30 minutes before cooking.

Place roast in a baking dish. Pour vegetable oil over meat, and then pour red wine into the dish.

Cook in a 450°F (230°C) oven for 15 minutes. After 15 minutes, reduce oven temperature to 300°F (150°C) and cook for 1 hour longer. After 1 hour, remove from oven, cover with aluminum foil, and let rest for 10 minutes before serving.

6

PORK ORLOFF

SERVES 6

Prep time: 25 minutes
Cook time: 45 minutes

INGREDIENTS

1 boneless pork roast (about 2-1/4 lbs)
1/4 cup (60 ml) wholegrain mustard
10 slices aged Gouda cheese
10 slices prosciutto
Salt and freshly ground pepper
4 leaves fresh sage, chopped
1/4 cup (60 ml) 35% cream
1/2 cup (125 ml) white wine

PREPARATION

Remove string from roast and cut roast crosswise into 1/2-inch slices. The slices should stay attached at the bottom for easy stuffing, and to prevent the cheese from melting out of the bottom. Brush the inside of each slice with wholegrain mustard. Insert a slice of cheese and a slice of prosciutto between each pork slice and then tie the roast lengthwise with kitchen string to pack the meat and fillings together as tightly as possible. Season with salt and pepper.

Place roast in an oiled roasting pan. In a small bowl, combine sage, cream, and white wine, and then pour mixture over roast. Cook in a 400°F (200°C) oven for 45 minutes, basting the roast with its cooking juices every 15 minutes. Serve with the side dish of your choice.

7

CORNISH HEN WITH GRAPES

SERVES 4

Prep time: 10 minutes
Cook time: 50 minutes

INGREDIENTS

2 Cornish game hens
1 red onion, thinly sliced
2 cups (500 ml) red seedless grapes
5 oz herb and garlic-flavored soft spread cheese
(such as Boursin)
1 tbsp olive oil
Salt and freshly ground pepper
1 tbsp honey
1 tsp sherry vinegar

PREPARATION

In a bowl, combine onion and grapes. Stuff game hen cavities with cheese (2-1/2 oz each) and onion and grape mixture. Using kitchen string, tie hen legs together to prevent the stuffing from spilling out.

Brush hens with oil and season with salt and pepper. Place in a roasting pan and cook in a 350°F (175°C) oven for 30 minutes. Meanwhile, combine honey and vinegar in a small bowl. After 30 minutes, remove pan from oven and pour honey and vinegar mixture over birds. Return to oven, roast for another 20 minutes, and serve (each hen serves 2).

DID YOU KNOW?

The Cornish game hen isn't a game bird; it's actually a type of chicken that, despite its name, can be male or female (defying the designation "hen," which is the common name for a female chicken), and has a plumper, rounder breast than a regular domestic chicken.

ROASTED MARROW ON TOAST

SERVES 4

Marinating time: 12 hours
Prep time: 5 minutes
Cook time: 30 minutes

INGREDIENTS

4 beef marrow bones
4 cloves garlic, crushed
4 sprigs fresh thyme
2 tbsp olive oil
4 slices country bread
Plain or flavored sea salt

PREPARATION

Soak bones in double their volume of water, in the refrigerator, for at least 12 hours.

Drain and dry marrow bones and place on a baking sheet. Cover the marrow at the center of each bone with a crushed garlic clove and a sprig of thyme. Pour olive oil over all and roast in a 400°F (200°C) for 30 minutes, or until a toothpick is easily inserted into the marrow.

Serve each marrow bone with a slice of toasted country bread and a bit of sea salt.

9

PORK & ROASTED PEACHES

SERVES 2 TO 4

Prep time: 15 minutes
Cook time: 15 minutes

INGREDIENTS

1 tbsp vegetable oil
1 pork loin
Salt and freshly ground pepper
3 peaches, pitted and quartered
1 tbsp butter
1/4 cup (60 ml) balsamic vinegar
1 tbsp honey
1/2 cup (60 ml) chicken stock
1 cinnamon stick
1 star anise

PREPARATION

In a large pan, heat oil over high heat. Season pork loin with salt and pepper and sear on all sides, until browned. Add peaches and butter and cook for 30 seconds. Deglaze with balsamic vinegar, add honey, and roll pork in the liquid to fully coat.

Transfer pork to a roasting pan. Pour chicken stock into the pan used to cook the pork and mix well, scraping up the brown bits at the bottom of the pan. Pour over pork loin and arrange peaches, cut sides up, around the meat. Add cinnamon stick and star anise. Roast in a 400°F (200°C) oven for 15 minutes and serve.

LAMB SHAWARMA

SERVES 8

TASTY TIP

If you don't have a grill rack for your grill pan, use thickly-sliced onions to raise your roast off of the bottom of the pan.

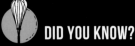

DID YOU KNOW?

Paper was extremely expensive during the Middle Ages, so parchment for writing was often made from the stretched skin of lambs.

Marinating time: 5 to 24 hours
Prep time: 20 minutes
Cook time: about 2 hours

1 semi-boneless leg of lamb, tied

FOR SHAWARMA SEASONING

1 tbsp each black peppercorns, ground coriander, cumin, mild paprika, and salt
4 cloves
1 tsp ground cardamom
1/2 tsp each cinnamon, grated nutmeg, ground ginger, and fenugreek
4 cloves garlic, chopped
Juice of 1 lemon
1/2 cup (125 ml) vegetable oil

FOR SERVING

12 pitas
2 onions, thinly sliced
6 tomatoes, cubed
1 bunch fresh cilantro, roughly chopped
1 bunch fresh mint, roughly chopped
Labneh cheese
Harissa sauce

PREPARATION

In a bowl, combine all shawarma seasoning ingredients.

Rub the entire leg of lamb with seasoning, wrap in plastic wrap, and refrigerate for 5 to 24 hours.

Place lamb in a roasting pan with a grill rack (if you don't have a grill rack, use thickly-sliced onions to raise the meat off of the bottom of a baking dish or roasting pan). Pour 1 inch of water into the pan. Cook lamb for 20 minutes per pound in a 400°F (200°C) oven, basting meat with its cooking juices every 20 minutes. There should always be 1 inch of liquid at the bottom of the pan, so add water as needed. After 1 hour, cover leg of lamb with aluminum foil to prevent spices from burning.

When the lamb has cooked for the required amount of time according to its weight, remove from oven and let rest for 15 minutes, covered in the aluminum foil.

Set a table with pitas, onions, tomatoes, fresh cilantro and mint, labneh, and harissa, and let everyone assemble their own succulent shawarmas. Perfect for fun, casual get-togethers with friends and family!

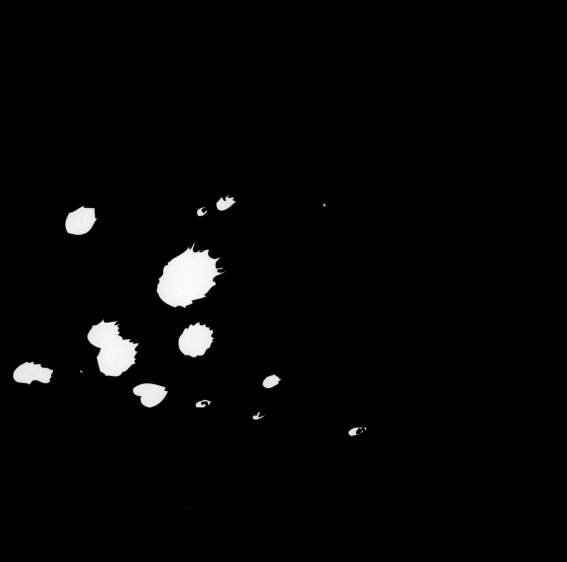

11

SWEET & NUTTY BRUSSELS SPROUTS

SERVES 4

Prep time: 10 minutes
Cook time: 20 minutes

INGREDIENTS

20 medium Brussels sprouts, halved
2 tbsp butter, melted
1 tbsp sugar
1/4 cup (60 ml) freshly pressed apple juice (not from concentrate)
Salt and freshly ground pepper
1/2 cup (125 ml) walnuts
1/4 cup (60 ml) fresh chives, chopped

PREPARATION

In a bowl, combine Brussels sprouts, melted butter, sugar, and apple juice. Season with salt and pepper and arrange on a baking sheet lined with parchment paper.

Roast in a 400°F (200°C) oven for 15 minutes. Add walnuts and chives, stir, and cook for another 5 minutes. Serve.

 **DID YOU KNOW?**

Up to 40 buds (the small, edible sprouts) can grow on just one of the plant's long, thick stalks!

BLUE CHEESE & APPLE PORK WELLINGTON

SERVES 2

TASTY TIP

If you prefer a milder flavor, use goat cheese instead of blue cheese, or omit the cheese altogether.

DID YOU KNOW?

The most popular theory suggests that this dish was named after Arthur Wellesley, 1st Duke of Wellington. Another theory claims it isn't named after the Duke himself: as the story goes, the cooked beef fillet was thought to resemble the shiny military boots worn, popularized by, and eventually named after, the famous Duke!

Prep time: 40 minutes
Cook time: 50 minutes

INGREDIENTS

Salt and freshly ground pepper
1 pork loin
2 tbsp vegetable oil
1 tbsp butter
2 apples, peeled, quartered, and very thinly sliced
1 clove garlic, finely chopped
2 tbsp blue cheese
4 slices prosciutto
1 square (1/2 package, about 1/2 lb) store-bought puff pastry
2 egg yolks, beaten

PREPARATION

Generously season pork loin with salt and pepper. In a pan, heat oil over high heat and sear pork on all sides, until browned. Remove from pan and let cool in the refrigerator.

In the same pan used to cook the pork, melt butter and sauté apples and garlic for 3 to 4 minutes, or until apples are nice and soft. Add blue cheese and stir to melt. Season with salt and pepper and let cool in the refrigerator.

Place a large piece of plastic wrap on a flat work surface. Line up prosciutto slices on the plastic wrap, side-by-side and slightly overlapping. Spread apples over half of the prosciutto and place the pork loin over apples. Using the plastic wrap as a guide, roll the pork and apples, wrapping them as tightly as possible in the prosciutto. Twist the ends of the plastic wrap to seal it completely and refrigerate for 15 minutes.

On a lightly-floured work surface, roll out puff pastry dough into a 16-inch x 8-inch rectangle. Unwrap prosciutto-wrapped tenderloin and set it in the center of the pastry. Brush pastry edges with egg yolk and then fold up the longer sides around the loin and trim the excess pastry at the four corners. Fold trimmed sides up to close, brush entire surface of pastry with egg, and then place on an oiled baking sheet, seam side down. With a small knife, slice small slits in the top of the pastry to allow steam to escape. Cook in a 175°C (350°F) oven for 30 minutes.

Let rest for 10 minutes and cut into fairly thick slices, about 1-1/2 inches each.

13

CLASSIC MEAT LOAF

SERVES 6

 **DID YOU KNOW?**

During the Great Depression, cereal grains were often added to meatloaf to stretch the meat *and* the food budget, and are now a conventional ingredient in most meatloaf recipes.

Prep time: 30 minutes
Cook time: 1 hour and 15 minutes

INGREDIENTS

1 onion, quartered
1 carrot, peeled and cut into pieces
8 button mushrooms
3 cloves garlic
1 tbsp olive oil
2-1/4 lbs ground beef
1/2 cup (125 ml) breadcrumbs
2 eggs
1 can (28 oz) crushed tomatoes
Salt and freshly ground pepper
8 slices bacon
2 tbsp brown sugar
1/2 cup (125 ml) water

PREPARATION

In a food processor, finely chop onion, carrot, mushrooms, and garlic. In a pan, heat olive oil and sauté vegetable mixture for 5 to 6 minutes.

In a large bowl, combine ground beef, breadcrumbs, eggs, vegetable mixture, and 1 cup (250 ml) of the canned crushed tomatoes. Season with salt and pepper and mix well. Using your hands, form a loaf with the meat mixture, about 12 inches x 3 inches.

Place meatloaf in a baking dish. Drape bacon slices, side-by-side and slightly overlapping, over the meatloaf, tucking the ends under the loaf. In a small bowl, dissolve brown sugar in 1 tbsp water. Brush bacon with this mixture and then pour remaining crushed tomatoes and water around the meatloaf.

Bake in a 400°F (200°C) oven for 1 hour and 15 minutes. When bacon is crispy, pour the tomato sauce in the dish over the entire meatloaf, slice, and serve.

14

SALT-CRUSTED SALMON & ASPARAGUS

SERVES 4

Prep time: 10 minutes
Cook time: 20 minutes

FOR SALT CRUST

3-1/2 lbs coarse salt
4 egg whites

FOR SALMON

20 asparagus stalks
2 cloves garlic, chopped
1 salmon fillet, with skin (about 2 lbs)

PREPARATION

In a large bowl, combine salt and egg whites.

With your hands, snap off the tough bottom ends of the asparagus (they will break naturally where the spears become tender).

Line a baking sheet with parchment paper and cover with a 1/4-inch layer of salt, pressing down firmly to compact. Place asparagus side-by-side on the salt and sprinkle with chopped garlic. Place salmon on top of asparagus, flesh side down. Cover entire salmon with remaining salt, pressing down firmly.

Cook in a 400°F (200°C) oven for 20 minutes. Break the crust and serve.

 **DID YOU KNOW?**

Much of the sea salt found in gourmet and specialty shops is cultivated naturally and harvested by hand by *sauniers*, who use traditional methods that date back to the Middle Ages.

PIRI-PIRI CHICKEN

SERVES 4

Marinating time: 4 to 12 hours
Prep time: 30 minutes
Cook time: 1 hour and 15 minutes

1 whole chicken

FOR PIRI-PIRI MARINADE

1/2 cup (125 ml) piri-piri sauce
1 onion, quartered
4 cloves garlic
Juice of 2 lemons
1 cup (250 ml) pale ale
2 tbsp sugar
1 tbsp salt
1/3 cup (80 ml) vegetable oil

PREPARATION

Place chicken on a work surface, breast down. Using a large, sharp knife, split the bird along the back by cutting along the spine. Turn the chicken over and flatten it. This technique is known as *en crapaudine*.

For piri-piri marinade: With a hand blender, purée all marinade ingredients until smooth. Place chicken in a large dish or container and pour marinade over chicken, making sure the entire bird is coated. Let marinate in the refrigerator for 4 to 12 hours.

Remove chicken from marinade and transfer to a baking sheet, breast side down. Transfer marinade to a small pot and let simmer over low heat for 20 minutes.

Roast chicken in a 400°F (200°C) oven for 30 minutes. After 30 minutes, flip chicken, brush with marinade, and cook for another 30 minutes. Brush one last time with marinade and finish roasting for 15 minutes. Cut chicken into pieces and serve with the side dishes of your choice.

DID YOU KNOW?

The piri-piri pepper, also called pili-pili or peri-peri depending on the region, is used to make the popular spicy Portuguese sauce of the same name. Pili-pili is actually Swahili for "pepper pepper."

16

SUNDAY SAUSAGE ROAST

SERVES 4

Prep time: 15 minutes
Cook time: 40 minutes

INGREDIENTS

6 sausages of your choice
16 button mushrooms
2 red peppers, seeded and cut into 1-inch strips
2 red onions, cut into 1/2-inch strips
1/4 cup (60 ml) balsamic vinegar
1/4 cup (60 ml) olive oil
Salt and freshly ground pepper
1/4 cup (60 ml) fresh parsley, chopped

PREPARATION

In a bowl, combine sausages, mushrooms, red peppers, onions, balsamic vinegar, and olive oil. Season with salt and pepper.

Transfer mixture to a roasting pan and cook in a 400°F (200°C) oven for 40 minutes. Sprinkle with fresh parsley and serve with Dijon mustard or dijonnaise.

TURKEY & CRANBERRY ROLL-UP

SERVES 6

Prep time: 40 minutes
Cook time: 1 hour and 25 minutes

FOR CRANBERRY GLAZE

2 tbsp butter
2 red onions, thinly sliced
1/4 cup (60 ml) canned or homemade cranberry sauce
1 tbsp red wine vinegar
1/2 cup (125 ml) port
2 leaves fresh sage
1 tsp salt
1 tsp freshly ground pepper

FOR TURKEY

2 tbsp vegetable oil
1 boneless turkey roast (about 3-1/2 lbs)
1 cup (250 ml) veal stock
1/4 cup (60 ml) 35% cream

PREPARATION

For cranberry glaze: In a pot, melt butter and sauté onions for 6 to 8 minutes. Add remaining glaze ingredients and let simmer for 10 to 15 minutes over low heat. With a hand blender, purée mixture until smooth and thick. Let cool.

For turkey: In a large pan, heat vegetable oil and sear turkey on all sides, until browned. Transfer to a roasting pan. Deglaze the pan used to cook the turkey with veal stock and then pour around turkey roast.

Brush turkey with glaze and roast in a 350°F (175°C) oven for 1 hour and 15 minutes, brushing it with another layer of glaze every 15 minutes. After removing turkey from oven, cover with aluminum foil and let rest for 10 minutes. Meanwhile, pour cooking juices into a small pot, add cream, and reduce until thick enough to coat the back of a spoon. Slice turkey and serve with sauce.

VEAL PROVENÇAL

SERVES 4

Prep time: 10 minutes
Cook time: 45 minutes

INGREDIENTS

1 top round veal roast (about 2-1/4 lbs)
Salt and freshly ground pepper
2 tbsp vegetable oil
1/2 cup (125 ml) white wine
2 shallots, thinly sliced
1/2 cup (125 ml) Kalamata olives, pitted
20 cherry tomatoes
2 tbsp fresh oregano, chopped
1/3 cup (80 ml) 35% cream

PREPARATION

Place veal in a roasting pan, season with salt and pepper, and pour vegetable oil over top. Cook in a 500°F (260°C) oven for 15 minutes, or until meat is nicely browned.

Remove from oven and add white wine. Scatter shallots, olives, tomatoes, and oregano around the roast. Return to oven and lower heat to 300°F (150°C). Cook for 20 minutes, basting the meat with its cooking juices halfway through. After 20 minutes, remove from oven and transfer meat to a plate. Cover with aluminum foil and let rest for 10 minutes. Pour cream into the roasting pan and return to oven, without the meat, and cook for another 10 minutes. Stir sauce and serve over sliced veal.

PORTOBELLO PORK ROAST

SERVES 4

Prep time: 20 minutes
Cook time: 1 hour and 10 minutes

INGREDIENTS

1 boneless pork roast (about 2-1/4 lbs)
Salt and freshly ground pepper
2 tbsp vegetable oil
2 shallots, thinly sliced
3 portobello mushrooms, thinly sliced
3/4 cup (180 ml) white wine
1 tbsp sherry vinegar
6 sprigs fresh thyme
1/2 cup (125 ml) 35% cream

PREPARATION

Season pork roast with salt and pepper. In a large pan, heat oil over high heat and sear roast on all sides, until browned. Transfer to a roasting pan.

In the same pan used to cook the pork, sauté shallots and mushrooms for 4 to 5 minutes. Deglaze with white wine and then pour mixture around pork. Add vinegar and thyme.

Roast in a 350°F (175°C) oven for 1 hour, basting the meat with its cooking juices every 20 minutes. After 1 hour, remove dish from oven and transfer pork roast to a plate. Let rest for 10 minutes.

Pour mushroom gravy into a small pot, stir in cream, and reduce until sauce is thick enough to coat the back of a spoon. Season with salt and pepper and serve with pork.

RUSSIAN ROAST BEEF

SERVES 4

Prep time: 15 minutes

INGREDIENTS

Roast beef, cooked (see recipe on page 132)
1 tbsp soy sauce
1/4 cup (60 ml) sour cream
1 tsp horseradish
Salt
1/4 tsp freshly ground pepper
2 pickled beets, cut into 1/2-inch cubes
1 shallot, thinly sliced
2 large dill pickles, chopped
2 tbsp chives, finely chopped

PREPARATION

Slice roast beef as thinly as possible and place on a serving plate. Brush with soy sauce and set aside.

In a bowl, combine sour cream, horseradish, salt, and pepper.

Top beef with sour cream sauce and then sprinkle with beets, shallot, pickles, and chives. Serve as an appetizer.

 **DID YOU KNOW?**

Japanese wasabi paste is made from the plant of the same name, also called Japanese horseradish. Because the root is so expensive, wasabi paste sold outside of Japan is often a mixture of horseradish, mustard, starch, and green food coloring.

ROASTED RED PEPPERS

SERVES 4 TO 6

Prep time: 20 minutes
Cook time: 20 minutes

FOR PEPPERS

2 red peppers
2 yellow peppers
1 tbsp vegetable oil

FOR CLASSIC VINAIGRETTE

1/4 cup (60 ml) olive oil
2 tbsp sherry vinegar
2 tbsp fresh parsley, chopped
2 tbsp fresh oregano, chopped
Salt and freshly ground pepper

PREPARATION

Rub entire surface of peppers with vegetable oil and place on a baking sheet. Broil for 5 minutes on each side, or until skin is charred and easy to remove.

Remove from oven, place in a bowl, and cover with plastic wrap. Let cool to room temperature.

With your hands, split peppers and carefully remove seeds and skin. Cut into 1/2-inch strips.

In a bowl, combine peppers and classic vinaigrette ingredients. Mix well and serve.

TASTY TIP

Marinated roasted red peppers will keep for several days in the refrigerator. They're a wonderful accompaniment for poultry or fish, and make a flavorful salad or burger topping. An all-around perfect condiment!

PEKING DUCK

SERVES 4

TASTY TIP

If possible, remove the covering from the refrigerated duck 4 hours before cooking. The skin will dry out slightly, allowing it to crisp up beautifully in the oven.

DID YOU KNOW?

Duck has been roasted in China since about the 5th century CE. Peking duck is now one of the country's national dishes.

Marinating time: 12 hours
Prep time: 20 minutes
Cook time: 1 hour and 30 minutes

1 whole duck

FOR DUCK BRINE

6 cups water
1 inch fresh ginger, peeled and chopped
1 cup (250 ml) soy sauce
1 tbsp whole peppercorns
2 bay leaves

FOR PEKING GLAZE

1/4 cup (60 ml) honey
2 tbsp soy sauce
2 tbsp rice vinegar
1 tsp ground coriander
2 tbsp fresh thyme, chopped
Juice and zest of 1/2 orange
2 cloves garlic, chopped

PREPARATION

In a bowl, combine all duck brine ingredients. Place the duck in a bowl or container just big enough to fit the bird. Pour marinade over top, making sure the duck is completely covered. Refrigerate overnight.

In a bowl, combine all Peking glaze ingredients.

After letting it marinate overnight, remove duck from marinade. Remove excess marinade from duck by patting it dry, and then place on a grill rack in a roasting pan. Pour 1/2 inch of water into the bottom of the pan, adding water as needed while the bird is cooking. Brush duck with glaze and cook in a 375°F (190°C) oven for 1 hour and 15 minutes to 1 hour and 30 minutes, brushing the bird with glaze every 15 minutes. Slice and serve.

CITRUSY BARBECUE SALMON

SERVES 4

FOR SALMON

1/2 salmon fillet, skin removed,
taken from the widest part of the fish
2 tbsp orange marmelade

FOR BARBECUE RUB

1 tbsp olive oil
1 tbsp brown sugar
2 tsp coarse salt
1 tsp freshly ground black pepper
1 tbsp mild paprika
1/2 tsp dry mustard
1/2 tsp onion powder
1/2 tsp garlic powder
1/4 tsp cayenne pepper

PREPARATION

In a bowl, combine all barbecue rub ingredients. Set aside.

Butterfly salmon fillet by slicing the fish along the side horizontally, without separating it completely. Open fillet like a book, brush the inside with marmelade, close, and roll up into a log. Tie up salmon roll, leaving about 2 inches between each string, rub with barbecue rub, and refrigerate for 30 minutes.

Place salmon in a lightly-oiled roasting pan and cook in a 400°F (200°C) oven for 20 minutes. Slice and serve with the side dish of your choice.

JERK CHICKEN

SERVES 4

Marinating time: 4 to 24 hours
Prep time: 15 minutes
Cook time: 30 minutes

8 chicken thighs, with skin

FOR JERK MARINADE

2 tsp allspice
1/2 tsp nutmeg, grated
1/2 tsp mace, grated
2 tsp salt
1 tbsp brown sugar
2 tsp fresh thyme
1 tsp freshly ground pepper
3 green onions, cut into pieces
1 habanero pepper (or Scotch Bonnet), seeded
2 cloves garlic
1/4 cup (60 ml) vegetable oil

PREPARATION

For jerk marinade: With a hand blender, or in a food processor, purée all marinade ingredients until smooth.

Combine chicken and marinade. Let marinate in the refrigerator for at least 4 hours, but for no more than 24 hours.

Place chicken on a lightly-oiled baking sheet and cook in a 400°F (200°C) oven for 30 minutes. Serve with French fries or roasted potatoes (see recipe on page 140).

 **DID YOU KNOW?**

Be careful when handling the habanero peppers! These small peppers are intensely spicy—so spicy, in fact, that they can irritate the skin on contact. Wear gloves, or make sure to wash your hands thoroughly afterwards.

PORK BELLY WITH MAPLE CALVADOS GLAZE

SERVES 8

Marinating time: 4 to 12 hours
Prep time: 1 hour
Cook time: 2 hours and 30 minutes

1 slab pork belly (about 2-1/4 lbs) with the rind (fat) still attached
12 new potatoes, halved

FOR MAPLE CALVADOS GLAZE

1/2 cup (125 ml) pure maple syrup
1/2 cup (125 ml) calvados
1/2 cup (125 ml) apple cider vinegar
1/2 cup (125 ml) freshly pressed apple juice
(not from concentrate)
2 tbsp brown sugar
2 tbsp Dijon mustard
1/4 cup (60 ml) soy sauce

PREPARATION

With a knife, make scores in the pork belly rind, about 1/4-inch apart, cutting down about halfway through the rind.

In a large bowl, combine all glaze ingredients. Place pork belly in the bowl, coat with glaze, and refrigerate overnight, or for at least 4 hours.

When it has finished marinating, remove pork belly from marinade. Pour marinade into a small pot and bring to a boil. Let simmer for 30 to 40 minutes over low heat, stirring occasionally, until the liquid has reduced by half. Refrigerate the glaze so that it continues to thicken.

Place pork belly in a roasting pan and cook in a 400°F (200°C) oven for 30 minutes. After 30 minutes, reduce oven temperature to 300°F (150°C) and cook for 2 hours longer.

When only 1 hour of cooking remains, arrange potatoes around the pork. During this last hour, brush pork belly generously with glaze every 15 minutes.

Slice and serve with potatoes. Pork belly is a decadent alternative to bacon, especially for brunch!

26

LEMONY CHICKEN & WILD MUSHROOMS

SERVES 4

Prep time: 10 minutes
Cook time: 1 hour and 20 minutes

INGREDIENTS

1 whole chicken
8 sprigs fresh thyme
12 cloves garlic, crushed
1 lemon, quartered
Salt and freshly ground pepper
2 tbsp olive oil
12 button mushrooms
2 cups (500 ml) wild mushrooms of your choice
(oyster, chanterelle, morel, shiitake, etc.)

PREPARATION

Stuff chicken cavity with thyme, garlic cloves, and lemon quarters.

Truss chicken with kitchen string. Season with salt and pepper, place in a roasting pan, and pour olive oil over top. Roast in a 400°F (200°C) oven for 1 hour, basting the bird with its cooking juices every 10 minutes. After 1 hour, scatter mushrooms around chicken and cook for another 20 minutes. Carve or cut into pieces and serve.

TASTY TIP

If you're in the mood for luxury, a small tin of foie gras is all you need! Just add it along with the stuffing ingredients; no need to spread it inside, as it will melt inside the bird and provide rich, decadent flavor.

27

BEST-EVER HONEY-GLAZED HAM

SERVES 12

INGREDIENTS

1/4 cup (60 ml) honey
1 cup (250 ml) apple juice
1/2 cup (125 ml) brown sugar
1/2 tsp ground cloves
1/2 tsp freshly ground pepper
2 bay leaves
1 bone-in pork shoulder picnic ham (about 6-1/2 lbs)
1 bottle (12 oz) dark beer

PREPARATION

In a small pot, combine honey, apple juice, and brown sugar. Add cloves, pepper, and bay leaf. Bring to a boil and let simmer for 8 to 10 minutes over low heat, or until the mixture becomes thick, with the texture of a caramel glaze.

With a small knife, score a diamond pattern in the fat on top of the ham.

Place ham in a roasting pan and pour beer over top. Brush with glaze.

Cover and cook in a 300°F (150°C) ovent for 1 hour and 30 minutes. After 1 hour and 30 minutes, remove cover and cook for 1 hour longer, basting ham often with its cooking juices and brushing it frequently with glaze. Slice and serve.

TASTY TIP

Roast your ham the French Canadian way by replacing the honey and brown sugar with 1 cup (250 ml) pure maple syrup!

DID YOU KNOW?

In the 1930s, popular ham glaze ingredients included ginger ale, marshmallows, pineapple, and pickle brine!

28

SUMMER VEGGIES

SERVES 6

Prep time: 20 minutes
Cook time: 20 minutes

INGREDIENTS

1 red pepper, seeded and cut into 1/2-inch strips
1 zucchini, seeded and cut into 1/2-inch rounds
8 asparagus spears, ends trimmed, cut into 3 pieces each
1 red onion, thinly sliced
2 tomatoes, cut into 1-inch cubes
2 cups (500 ml) eggplant, cut into 1-inch cubes
4 cloves garlic, chopped
1/4 cup (60 ml) olive oil
2 tbsp balsamic vinegar
Zest of 1 lemon
2 tbsp fresh oregano, chopped
Salt and freshly ground pepper

PREPARATION

In a bowl, combine all ingredients. Mix well.

Transfer to a baking sheet and cook in a 400°F (200°C) oven for 20 minutes. Serve as a side dish.

KARATE QUAIL!

SERVES 3

 TASTY TIP

If the quail legs are browning too quickly, cover them with aluminum foil. This way, the breasts will become nicely golden and the legs won't burn.

 **DID YOU KNOW?**

The French term for breeding quail, *coturni-culture*, is taken from the Latin name for a particular kind of quail, the *coturnix*. No word for this practice exists in English!

Marinating time: 4 to 12 hours
Prep time: 10 minutes
Cook time: 30 minutes

FOR SAKE MARINADE

1 cup (250 ml) sake
1/2 cup (125 ml) soy sauce
3/4 cup (180 ml) mirin

FOR QUAIL

6 quails
12 baby bok choy
1 tbsp vegetable oil
Salt and freshly ground pepper
2 tbsp sesame seeds, toasted

PREPARATION

In a large bowl, combine all sake marinate ingredients. Add quails and coat with marinade. Let marinate in the refrigerator for 4 to 12 hours.

In a bowl, combine bok choy and oil. Season with salt and pepper and set aside.

Place quails in a large roasting pan and cook in a 400°F (200°C) oven for 20 minutes. Baste with cooking juices and then arrange bok choy around quails. Cook for 10 minutes longer. Sprinkle with sesame seeds and serve.

RUSTIC ROAST BEEF SANDWICH

SERVES 1

Prep time: 10 minutes
Cook time: 5 minutes

INGREDIENTS

1 tbsp olive oil
1 portobello mushroom, chopped
1 tbsp fresh chives, finely chopped
1 tbsp cream cheese
1 tsp wholegrain mustard
1 ciabatta bun
Roast beef, cooked (see recipe on page 132)
A few slices tomato
A few leaves lettuce

PREPARATION

Thinly slice roast beef.

In a pan, heat oil and sauté portobello mushroom for 3 to 4 minutes. Set aside.

In a small bowl, combine chives, cream cheese, mustard, and sautéed mushrooms. Mix well.

Cut bun in half and spread each half with cream cheese mixture. Top with beef, tomato slices, and lettuce leaves. Close sandwich and enjoy.

TASTY TIP

This sandwich is delicious cold, but if you like, broil the cream cheese-topped ciabatta halves for just a few minutes to crisp up the bread and turn the cheese into a warm, luscious spread.

31

ROASTED GARLIC BUTTER

MAKES 20 ROSETTES

DID YOU KNOW?

Instead of costly medicinal herbs and spices, Medieval peasants used garlic as a preventative medicine and a cure-all; it was worn around the neck or chewed to combat plague, braided and hung in doorways to prevent evil spirits from entering homes, made into poultices to heal corns, warts, insect and snake bites, and used to fight rheumatism, parasites, and jaundice.

Louis Pasteur was the first to tout garlic's anti-bacterial properties. It was used during World War I to fight gangrene and septicaemia, and the British government even offered money for garlic to be used in hospitals.

Prep time: 30 minutes
Cook time: 40 minutes

FOR ROASTED GARLIC

4 heads garlic
1/3 cup (80 ml) olive oil

FOR GARLIC BUTTER

Roasted garlic (see recipe above)
1 lb (16 oz) butter
1/2 cup (125 ml) fresh Parmesan cheese, grated
1/2 cup (125 ml) fresh parsley, chopped

PREPARATION

For roasted garlic: Brush a baking sheet with 2 tbsp olive oil. With a knife, cut off the bottoms of the garlic heads, making sure the cloves don't separate. Place garlic heads, cut sides down, on the oiled baking sheet and drizzle generously with remaining olive oil. Roast in a 250°F (120°C) oven for 40 minutes; garlic should be golden brown but not charred. Remove from oven and let cool, and then squeeze out roasted garlic cloves.

For garlic butter: In a food processor, or using a fork, combine roasted garlic, butter, and Parmesan cheese. Blend well for a uniform mixture. Add parsley at the end and quickly mix to combine.

Transfer to a pastry bag and, on a baking sheet, pipe into rosettes (about 1 to 2 tbsp each). Chill in the freezer or in the refrigerator. Once the rosettes have hardened, transfer to a freezer bag and store in the freezer to use later.

Serve your elegant rosettes with fresh bread, on toast, with vegetables, or with a nice steak or piece of fish... garlic butter makes everything taste better!

32

TROUT WITH SUNNY SALSA

SERVES 4

Prep time: 25 minutes
Cook time: 15 minutes

FOR MANGO SALSA

1 mango, peeled and cut into 1/2-inch cubes
1 tomato, cut into 1/2-inch cubes
2 tbsp sweet Thai chili sauce
1 tsp red wine vinegar
1 tbsp olive oil
Salt and freshly ground pepper
1/4 cup (60 ml) fresh cilantro, chopped

FOR TROUT

2 whole trout, without heads, cleaned and boned
Salt and freshly ground pepper
1/2 cup (125 ml) cornmeal
2 lemons, sliced into rounds
1/4 cup (60 ml) olive oil

PREPARATION

In a bowl, combine all mango salsa ingredients. Set aside.

Season the inside of each trout with salt and pepper. Dredge in cornmeal, shaking off any excess. Place lemon slices in the trout. Pour a bit of olive oil onto a baking sheet, place fish on the oil, and pour remaining oil over top of fish. Cook in a 400°F (200°C) oven for 15 minutes. Serve with mango salsa.

THE ORIGINAL ROASTED CHICKEN

SERVES 4

TASTY TIP

The best way to get extra crispy skin is to slide your fingers carefully under the bird's breast and leg skin to loosen the meat. It works every time!

Brining your turkey beforehand isn't absolutely necessary, but if you do have the time to do it, this extra step will make the bird incredibly juicy and tender.

Marinating time: 8 hours
Prep time: 25 minutes
Cook time: 1 hour and 15 minutes

FOR CHICKEN BRINE

8 cups water
1/2 cup (125 ml) coarse salt
1/3 cup (80 ml) sugar
2 bay leaves
1 tbsp coriander seeds
1 tbsp whole peppercorns
1 tbsp mustard seeds

INGREDIENTS

1 whole chicken
2 onions, quartered
4 cloves garlic
4 sprigs fresh thyme
1 tsp mild paprika
1 tbsp olive oil
1/2 tsp salt
2 carrots, peeled and cut into medium rounds
4 stalks celery, cut into pieces
8 new potatoes, halved
Salt and freshly ground pepper
1/4 cup (60 ml) water

PREPARATION

In a large pot, combine all chicken brine ingredients. Bring to a boil and remove from heat. Let cool to room temperature before adding chicken. Immerse chicken completely in brine and refrigerate for at least 8 hours.

After soaking for at least 8 hours, take chicken out of brine and remove excess brine by patting chicken dry. Place onions, garlic, and thyme in the chicken cavity. In a small bowl, combine paprika, olive oil, and salt. Rub entire surface of chicken with this mixture.

Place carrots, celery, and potatoes in a roasting pan. Season with salt and pepper, add water, and place chicken in the middle of the pan.

Cover and cook in a in a 350°F (175°C) oven for 30 minutes. After 30 minutes, remove cover and continue cooking for 45 minutes, basting the bird with its cooking juices every 15 minutes. Cut into pieces, or carve, and serve.

PULLED PORK

SERVES 8

Prep time: 15 minutes
Cook time: 4 hours

1 pork shoulder (about 3-1/2 lbs)

FOR SMOKY SEASONING

2 tbsp salt
1/4 cup (60 ml) sugar
1 tbsp mild paprika
2 tbsp chili powder
1 tbsp garlic powder
1 tbsp dry mustard
1 tbsp fresh thyme, chopped
1 tsp liquid smoke
1/4 cup (60 ml) vegetable oil

PREPARATION

In a bowl, combine all seasoning ingredients. Rub pork shoulder with this mixture, and then place in a roasting pan. Cover and cook in a 300°F (175°C) oven for 2 hours. After 2 hours, remove cover and cook for 1 hour longer.

Shred pork using two forks. Serve pulled pork in sandwiches or in tacos, with French fries, or with whatever side dish you're craving at the moment!

FILET MIGNON & BÉARNAISE SAUCE

SERVES 4

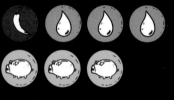

DID YOU KNOW?

One of the classic French sauces, béarnaise was first made in 1836 to mark the opening of Le Pavillon Henri IV, a restaurant outside of Paris named after the king, noted for his gourmet tastes.

Prep time: 20 minutes
Cook time: 40 minutes

FOR BEEF TENDERLOIN

1 beef tenderloin fillet (about 1-3/4 lbs), barded with pork fat (ask your butcher) and tied with string
2 tbsp steak spice
1/2 tsp salt
2 tbsp vegetable oil

FOR BÉARNAISE SAUCE

1/4 cup (60 ml) white wine vinegar
1/4 cup (60 ml) white wine
2 shallots, finely chopped
1/2 tsp whole peppercorns
2 sprigs fresh tarragon
4 egg yolks
3/4 cup (180 ml) butter, melted and then brought to room temperature
2 tbsp fresh tarragon, chopped
Salt and freshly ground pepper

PREPARATION

For beef tenderloin: Rub beef tenderloin with steak spice and salt. In a large pan, heat oil over high heat and sear meat on all sides, until browned. Cook in a 300°F (150°C) oven for 30 minutes, or until a meat thermometer inserted into the center of the meat reaches 120°F (50°C). Remove from oven, cover with aluminum foil, and let rest for 10 minutes.

For béarnaise sauce: In a small pan, bring vinegar, wine, shallots, peppercorns, and tarragon to a boil. Reduce until about 3 tbsp of liquid remain. Strain with a wire mesh strainer.

In a bowl, over a bain-marie, combine wine reduction and egg whites, whisking constantly, until sauce becomes thick and frothy.

Remove bowl from bain-marie. Off of the heat, add melted butter in a slow, steady stream, whisking vigorously. Add tarragon and season with salt and pepper. If sauce is too thick, add a bit of hot water. Keep at room temperature until it's time to serve. Serve filet mignon with béarnaise sauce.

36

ROASTED CARROTS

SERVES 4

Prep time: 10 minutes
Cook time: 15 minutes

INGREDIENTS

20 carrots, with stalks
2 tbsp honey
1 tbsp apple cider vinegar
2 tbsp butter
Salt and freshly ground pepper

PREPARATION

Peel carrots and trim stalks to about 1 inch long each. Place in a large bowl.

In a small bowl, combine honey, vinegar, and butter. Heat for 20 seconds in the microwave and mix well. Pour over carrots, season with salt and pepper, and toss to coat. Arrange carrots on a baking sheet lined with parchment paper and roast in a 400°F (200°C) oven for 15 minutes. Serve.

TASTY TIP

A recipe doesn't have to be time-consuming to be delicious! Sprinkle a bit of cumin or ginger into your sweet, buttery honey glaze, or try this simple side dish with fresh beets instead, peeled and cut into equal pieces. The cooking time will be slightly longer, and the oven temperature will be slightly lower: roast for about 30 minutes, in a 350°F (175°C) oven.

37

WORLD-FAMOUS BARBECUE CHICKEN

SERVES 4

Prep time: 10 minutes
Cook time: 1 hour and 20 minutes

FOR CHICKEN

1 whole chicken
3 tbsp barbecue seasoning (see recipe below)
2 tbsp vegetable oil
2 onions, quartered

FOR BARBECUE SEASONING

1/4 cup (60 ml) mild paprika
1 tbsp freshly ground pepper
1 tbsp celery salt
1 tbsp brown sugar
1 tsp dry mustard
1 tsp onion powder
1 tsp garlic powder
1 tsp cayenne pepper

PREPARATION

For barbecue seasoning: In a bowl, combine all ingredients. This blend will keep for 3 to 4 months, stored in the freezer in an airtight container.

Start by carefully sliding your fingers under the breast and leg skin to loosen it from the meat. This will result in wonderfully crispy skin.

In a small bowl, combine 3 tbsp barbecue seasoning and vegetable oil. Thoroughly rub entire chicken with this mixture, and then stuff chicken cavity with quartered onions.

Place chicken in a roasting pan and cook in a 400°F (200°C) oven for 1 hour and 20 minutes, basting it with its cooking juices half-way through. Carve, or cut into pieces, and serve.

 **DID YOU KNOW?**

Celery salt is a combination of salt and dried and ground celery seeds. This savory seasoning is a popular cocktail ingredient, and can be used as a substitute for regular table salt.

RIBS WITH BOURBON BARBECUE SAUCE

SERVES 4

Marinating time: 12 hours
Prep time: 45 minutes
Cook time: 2 hours

2 slabs pork spareribs
1 cup (250 ml) homemade or store-bought barbecue sauce

FOR RIB BRINE

4 cups water
1/2 cup (125 ml) salt
1/3 cup (80 ml) sugar
2 tbsp whole peppercorns
4 sprigs fresh thyme
2 bay leaves
24 ice cubes

FOR BOURBON BARBECUE SAUCE

1 onion, thinly sliced
4 cloves garlic, thinly sliced
1/2 cup (125 ml) bourbon
2 cups (500 ml) ketchup
1/3 cup (80 ml) red wine vinegar
1/4 cup (60 ml) Worcestershire sauce
3/4 cup (180 ml) brown sugar
3/4 cup (180 ml) molasses
1/4 cup (60 ml) tomato paste
2 tsp liquid smoke
1 tsp salt
1 tsp freshly ground pepper
1 tsp Tabasco sauce

PREPARATION

To make the brine, place all brine ingredients, except ice cubes, in a large pot. Bring to a boil, reduce heat to low, and let simmer for 5 minutes. After 5 minutes, remove from heat, add ice cubes, and mix well. If brine is still warm, refrigerate until cool. Cut each slab of ribs in half and immerse completely in brine. Refrigerate for at least 12 hours.

In a pan, cook onion, garlic, and bourbon for 10 minutes, or until onion is soft. Add remaining sauce ingredients and cook for 20 minutes, stirring occasionally to prevent sauce from sticking. Strain with a wire mesh strainer.

To cook ribs, remove from brine and dry thoroughly. Place on a grill rack in a roasting pan, and pour 1 inch water in the bottom of the pan. Cover and cook in a 300°F (150°C) oven for 1 hour. After 1 hour, remove cover, brush ribs generously with barbecue sauce, and raise oven temperature to 350°F (175°C). Cook ribs for 1 hour longer, brushing with sauce every 30 minutes.

Serve with the side dish of your choice.

39

RACK OF LAMB & PERSILLADE

SERVES 4

TASTY TIP

Finely chop a few sundried tomatoes and add to your persillade for a summery kick!

DID YOU KNOW?

The Ancient Greeks sacrificed black lambs to the "destructive winds" in return for favorable winds during long sea voyages.

Prep time: 15 minutes
Cook time: 25 minutes

FOR LAMB

2 racks of lamb
2 tbsp vegetable oil
Salt and freshly ground pepper
2 tbsp Dijon mustard

FOR PERSILLADE

1/4 cup (60 ml) fresh parsley, finely chopped
2 tbsp fresh thyme, finely chopped
2 tbsp fresh Parmesan cheese, grated
1/4 cup (60 ml) breadcrumbs
Salt and freshly ground pepper
2 cloves garlic, finely chopped
2 tbsp olive oil

PREPARATION

To start, and for a beautiful presentation, use a small knife to trim the excess fat and meat from the exposed bones, scraping in between each bone and removing the sinew and the nerve at the top of each piece.

In a large pan, heat oil over high heat. Season lamb with salt and pepper and place in the oil, fleshy side down. Use tongs to turn lamb, but only once the bottom is nicely browned.

Transfer to a baking dish and roast in a 400°F (200°C) oven for 8 minutes.

In a bowl, combine all persillade ingredients.

After 8 minutes, remove lamb from oven, brush with Dijon mustard, and firmly press a thick layer of persillade onto the top of the meat, making sure it sticks. Return to oven and cook for 10 minutes. Let rest for 5 minutes before serving.

40

MONKFISH, TAPENADE & PROSCIUTTO

SERVES 3

Marinating time: 1 hour
Prep time: 40 minutes
Cook time: 20 minutes

FOR MONKFISH

3 monkfish fillets (about 2 lbs total), cleaned and boned
5 slices (about 3 oz) prosciutto

FOR TAPENADE

2 cloves garlic, chopped
1/2 cup (125 ml) Kalamata olives, rinsed and pitted
2 tbsp capers, rinsed
4 drops Tabasco sauce
1/3 cup (80 ml) olive oil
Zest of 1 lemon
Freshly ground pepper

PREPARATION

In a food processor, purée all tapenade ingredients until smooth.

Coat monkfish fillets with tapenade and refrigerate for 1 hour.

Place a sheet of plastic wrap on a flat work surface, with the long side facing you. Place the prosciutto slices vertically, side-by-side and slightly overlapping, on top of the plastic wrap. Place the monkfish fillets at the bottom of and perpendicular to the prosciutto slices, at the end closest to you. Using the plastic wrap as a guide, roll up monkfish in the prosciutto to form a compact log. Discard plastic wrap.

Place on a lightly oiled baking sheet, seam side down. Cook in a 350°F (175°C) oven for 20 minutes. Slice and serve.

DID YOU KNOW?

Fishmongers almost never sell whole monkfish for one very obvious reason: it's extremely ugly, and nobody would buy it! In fact, before it became a popular cooking fish, fishermen would simply throw it back into the water; it was believed that monkfish were monsters that would bring bad luck.

41

ROASTED SQUASH & HUMMUS

SERVES 4

Prep time: 10 minutes
Cook time: 20 minutes

FOR SQUASH

1 butternut squash, peeled and seeded
2 tbsp butter, melted
1 tbsp honey
2 tbsp za'atar
Salt and freshly ground pepper

FOR HUMMUS

3 cloves garlic, crushed
1 can (19 oz) chickpeas, drained and rinsed
2 tbsp tahini
1/2 cup (125 ml) olive oil
Juice of 1 lemon
Salt and freshly ground pepper

PREPARATION

For squash: Cut squash into 2-inch x 1-inch pieces.

In a small bowl, melt butter and honey together in the microwave for about 20 seconds.

In a large bowl, toss squash in butter and honey mixture. Add za'atar, season with salt and pepper, and mix well. Arrange on a baking sheet lined with parchment paper.

Roast in a 400°F (200°C) oven for 15 minutes. Serve with home-made or store-bought hummus.

For hummus: In a pan, heat 2 tbsp of the olive oil and sauté garlic for 2 to 3 minutes over low heat. In a deep bowl, combine all ingredients and purée with a hand blender. Season with salt and pepper.

 **DID YOU KNOW?**

Tahini is also served as a dessert, with molasses, honey, or date syrup, and is used as the base for *halva*, a dense, sweet Middle Eastern dessert.

42

FOUR ALARM CHICKEN WINGS

SERVES 4

Marinating time: 2 to 12 hours
Prep time: 10 minutes
Cook time: 1 hour

24 chicken wings

FOR SPICY SAUCE

1/4 cup (60 ml) ketchup
2 tbsp white vinegar
2 tbsp sugar
1/4 cup (60 ml) hot sauce of your choice
(sriracha, piri-piri, sambal oelek, etc.)
1 tbsp steak spice

PREPARATION

In a large bowl, combine wings and spicy sauce ingredients. Let marinate in the refrigerator for at least 2 hours.

Place wings on an oiled baking sheet and cook in a 400°F (200°C) oven for 20 minutes. After 20 minutes, flip wings and cook for another 20 minutes. Flip one last time and cook for 20 minutes longer.

Serve with a side of sour cream flavored with a bit of onion powder and fresh herbs of your choice.

43

TRADITIONAL ROAST BEEF

SERVES 6

Prep time: 10 minutes
Cook time: 1 hour and 15 minutes

INGREDIENTS

1 onion, finely chopped
4 sprigs fresh thyme, leaves removed
2 tbsp Dijon mustard
1 tbsp Worcestershire sauce
Salt and freshly ground pepper
1 cut of quality roasting beef (about 4-1/2 lbs)
2 tbsp vegetable oil
1/2 cup (125 ml) red wine
1 cup (250 ml) water

PREPARATION

In a bowl, combine onion, thyme, mustard, Worcestershire, salt, and pepper. Rub entire surface of roast with this mixture. Place roast in a baking dish. Pour vegetable oil over meat and then pour red wine and water around it.

Roast in a 450°F (230°C) oven for 15 minutes. After 15 minutes, reduce oven temperature to 300°F (150°C) and cook for another 50 minutes, or until a meat thermometer inserted into the center of the meat reaches 130°F (55°C). Baste the roast with its cooking juices every 30 minutes.

After removing meat from oven, cover with aluminum foil and let rest for 10 to 15 minutes before serving.

 DID YOU KNOW?

In England, roast beef is usually served with Yorkshire pudding, which isn't a pudding in the classic sense. It's a bread-like side dish made from batter and used to soak up gravy.

BACON-WRAPPED RABBIT

SERVES 2 TO 4

TASTY TIP

For a creamy sauce to accompany this dish, keep the rabbit's cooking juices, add 1/4 cup (60 ml) 35% cream and the juice of 1/2 lemon. Season with salt and pepper and spoon generously over each serving.

DID YOU KNOW?

How to prepare a rabbit:

1. Using a very sharp knife, or a pair of kitchen scissors, cut the rabbit in half, between the ribcage and the saddle (or loin).

2. Cut off hind legs.

3. Cut saddle into 3 pieces.

4. Cut off front legs and discard ribcage.

After cutting, you will have 7 rabbit pieces: two hind legs, three saddle pieces, and two front legs.

Marinating time: 2 to 12 hours
Prep time: 30 minutes
Cook time: 45 minutes

FOR SUNDRIED TOMATO MARINADE

1 tbsp sherry vinegar
4 cloves garlic
4 anchovy fillets
4 green onions
8 sundried tomatoes
1 tbsp Dijon mustard
1/3 cup (80 ml) olive oil
Salt and freshly ground pepper
1 tsp sugar

FOR RABBIT

1 whole rabbit, cut into 7 pieces (see "Did you know?" sidebar)
14 slices bacon

PREPARATION

In a food processor, combine all sundried tomato marinade ingredients. Transfer to a bowl, add rabbit, and mix to coat. Cover and refrigerate for 2 to 12 hours.

On a work surface, roll each marinated rabbit piece in 2 slices bacon. Place in a roasting pan, seam sides down, and cook in a 350°F (175°C) oven for 45 minutes and serve.

COD WITH CLAM SAUCE

SERVES 4

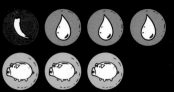

Prep time: 15 minutes
Cook time: 15 minutes

FOR COD FILLET

1 cod fillet (about 2 lbs), with skin
Salt and freshly ground pepper
1 tbsp flour
2 tbsp olive oil

FOR CLAM SAUCE

1 tbsp butter
2 shallots, finely chopped
20 clams, cleaned
1/2 cup (125 ml) white wine
1/2 cup (125 ml) 35% cream
8 leaves fresh sorrel, thinly sliced
Salt and freshly ground pepper

PREPARATION

Generously season the flesh side of the cod fillet. Sprinkle cod skin with flour, shaking off any excess. Place fillet, flesh side down, on a lightly oiled baking sheet. Lightly oil skin. Cook in a 400°F (200°C) oven for 20 minutes.

While the fish is cooking, melt butter in a small pot and sauté shallots for 3 to 4 minutes. Add clams, white wine, and cream. Cover and cook for 5 to 6 minutes. When the clams start to open, add sorrel and season with salt and pepper. Remove from heat when clamshells are fully open.

Serve fish with clam sauce.

DID YOU KNOW?

In the past, Northern European sailors would use cod liver oil to protect their skin from the sun.

46

ROASTED POTATOES

SERVES 4

 TASTY TIP

These spicy home fries pair perfectly with a creamy homemade mayonnaise! Or, for a sweet and savory treat, substitute the Yukon Gold potatoes with sweet potatoes, but cut the sugar from the recipe or they will be much too sweet.

 DID YOU KNOW?

The earliest evidence of humans cultivating potatoes was found in the Andes mountains, and dates back to 8,000 BCE. The potato was only introduced to Europe in the 16th century, after the discovery of North America.

Prep time: 10 minutes
Cook time: 30 minutes

INGREDIENTS

6 Yukon Gold potatoes, cut into 4 wedges each
1/4 cup (60 ml) olive oil
1 tsp mild paprika
1 tsp dried oregano
1/2 tsp freshly ground pepper
Zest of 1 lemon
1/2 tsp cayenne pepper
1 tsp salt
1 tsp sugar

PREPARATION

In a large bowl, combine all ingredients.

Spread potato wedges evenly on a baking sheet lined with parchment paper. Roast in a 400°F (200°C) oven for 30 minutes. Serve.

47

PORK ROAST & MELT-IN-YOUR-MOUTH POTATOES

SERVES 6

Prep time: 20 minutes
Cook time: 3 hours

INGREDIENTS

1 pork shoulder roast, tied (about 3-1/2 lbs)
4 cloves garlic
2 tbsp sugar
1 tbsp salt
1/2 tsp freshly ground black pepper
1 tbsp dry mustard
1 tbsp vegetable oil
4 Yukon Gold potatoes, peeled and cut into 6 pieces each

PREPARATION

Make 4 scores in the pork roast. Insert garlic cloves into scores.

In a small bowl, combine sugar, salt, pepper, mustard, and vegetable oil. Thoroughly rub pork with this mixture.

Transfer roast to a Dutch oven. Cover and cook in a 300°F (150°C) oven for 2 hours.

After 2 hours, remove cover and place potatoes in the cooking fat around the roast. Raise oven temperature to 350°F (175°C) and cook, uncovered, for 1 hour longer. Serve.

48

BEEF & RED WINE MARINADE

SERVES 6

Marinating time: 6 to 12 hours
Prep time: 10 minutes
Cook time: 4 hours

1 beef shoulder roast (about 3-1/2 lbs)

FOR RED WINE MARINADE

2 sprigs fresh rosemary, leaves removed
2 cloves garlic, thinly sliced
1/2 cup (125 ml) red wine
2 tbsp red wine vinegar
1 tbsp sugar
1/2 tsp freshly ground pepper
1/4 cup (60 ml) olive oil
1/2 tsp salt

PREPARATION

In a dish, combine all red wine marinade ingredients. In the same dish, coat beef in marinade and refrigerate for 6 to 12 hours.

Place roast in a baking dish and pour leftover marinade over top. Cover and cook in a 300°F (150°C) oven for 4 hours. Serve.

LEMON & OLIVE LAMB

SERVES 4

Prep time: 15 minutes
Cook time: 3 hours

INGREDIENTS

1 tbsp Dijon mustard
2 tbsp brown sugar
1 tsp salt
1/2 tsp freshly ground pepper
1 bone-in shoulder of lamb
4 sprigs rosemary
1 head garlic, halved
1 lemon, halved
1/2 cup (125 ml) white wine
1 cup (125 ml) small black olives

PREPARATION

In a small bowl, combine mustard, brown sugar, salt, and pepper. Brush meat with this mixture.

Place rosemary, garlic, and lemon halves in a small pile in the center of a baking dish and put shoulder of lamb on top. Pour in wine and olive oil and scatter olives around lamb.

Cover and cook in a 300°F (150°C) for 2 hours. After 2 hours, remove cover and cook for 1 more hour. Serve with cooking juices as a gravy.

SWEET POTATOES, APPLES & PECANS

SERVES 4

Prep time: 10 minutes
Cook time: 25 minutes

INGREDIENTS

1 large sweet potato, peeled and cut into 1-inch cubes
2 apples, cut into 1-inch cubes
1 tsp cumin
2 tbsp apple cider vinegar
1/4 cup (60 ml) freshly pressed apple juice (not from concentrate)
2 tbsp butter, melted
Salt and freshly ground pepper
1/4 cup (60 ml) pecans, roughly chopped
1/4 cup (60 ml) fresh parsley, chopped

PREPARATION

In a large bowl, combine all ingredients, except pecans and parsley. Season with salt and pepper and mix well.

Spread mixture evenly onto a baking sheet lined with parchment paper.

Cook in a 400°F (200°C) oven, on the center rack, for 20 minutes. After 20 minutes, remove from oven, add pecans, mix well, and cook for another 5 minutes. Sprinkle with parsley and serve.

TASTY TIP

This is the perfect side dish for Pork Orloff (see recipe on page 044)!

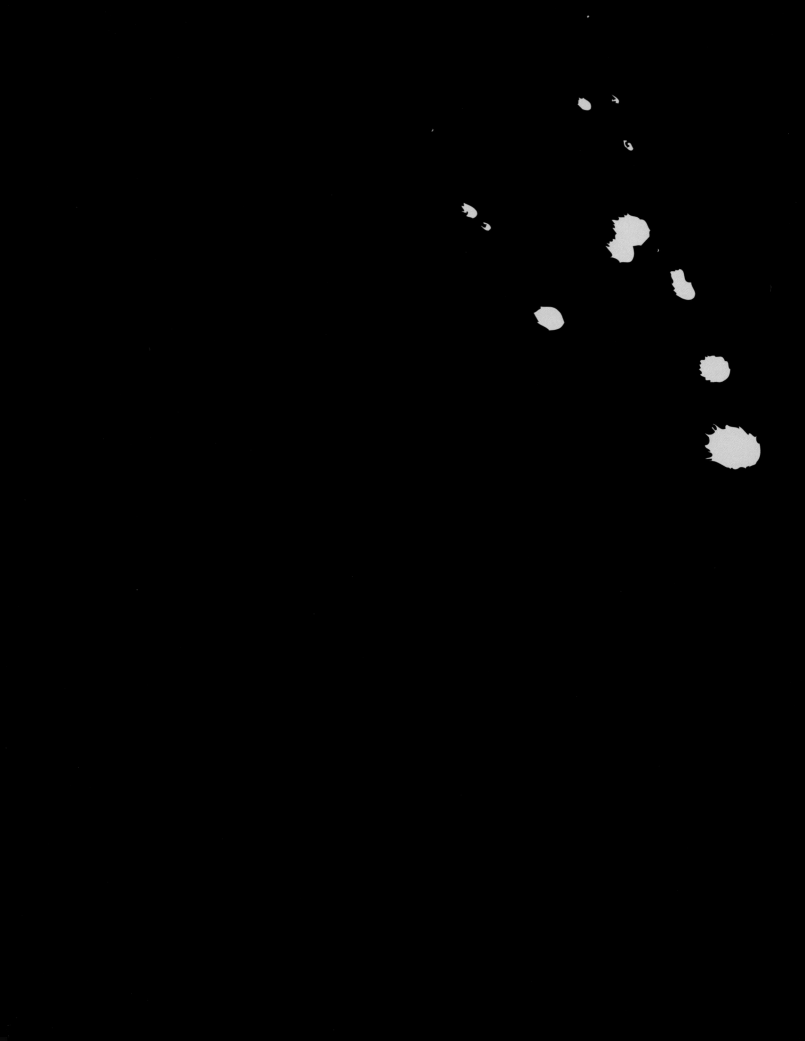

TANDOORI CHICKEN DRUMSTICKS

SERVES 4

DID YOU KNOW?

The name of this Indian dish comes from the traditional cylindrical clay oven used to cook it, the *tandoor*. The temperature in a *tandoor* can reach up to 903°F (485°C)!

Marinating time: 4 to 12 hours
Prep time: 40 minutes
Cook time: 30 minutes

8 chicken drumsticks

FOR TANDOORI MARINADE

1/2 cup (125 ml) plain yogurt
Juice of 1 lemon
1/4 cup (60 ml) olive oil
2 tbsp store-bought tandoori spice blend
1 tsp red food coloring

FOR MANGO CHUTNEY

1 tbsp vegetable oil
1 clove garlic, chopped
1 inch fresh ginger, peeled and chopped
1 mango, peeled and cut into 1/2-inch cubes
1/4 cup (60 ml) sugar
1/4 cup (60 ml) white vinegar
1 cinnamon stick
2 cloves
1 pinch crushed red pepper flakes
Salt and freshly ground pepper

PREPARATION

For tandoori marinade: In a bowl, combine all marinade ingredients. Add chicken drumsticks and coat in marinade. Let marinate in the refrigerator for at least 4 hours.

For mango chutney: Heat vegetable oil in a small pot and sauté garlic and ginger for 2 to 3 minutes. Add remaining ingredients, cover, and cook for 15 minutes over low heat. Remove cover and cook for 10 to 15 minutes longer, or until thick. Let cool before serving.

Place chicken on a lightly oiled baking sheet and cook in a 400°F (200°C) oven for 30 minutes.

Serve drumsticks with mango chutney and rice or naan bread.

HASSELBACK POTATOES

SERVES 4

Prep time: 45 minutes
Cook time: 1 hour and 25 minutes

INGREDIENTS

4 Russet potatoes, peeled
1 tbsp butter, melted
2 tbsp 35% cream
2 tbsp fresh Parmesan cheese, grated
1 tbsp fresh thyme, chopped
1/4 tsp sea salt
Freshly ground pepper

PREPARATION

Cut a thin slice off of the bottom of each potato to create a stable base. Insert a skewer through the length of each potato, about 1/2 inch from the bottom, to prevent you from cutting all the way through when slicing.

Cut thin slices (about 1/8 inch thick each) across the entire length of the potato. Remove skewers and soak potatoes in a bowl of cold water for at least 30 minutes. Drain and rinse well.

Pat potatoes dry and place on a baking sheet. Bake in a 350°F (175°C) oven for 15 minutes. After 15 minutes, brush with melted butter and bake for another 40 minutes.

Meanwhile, combine cream, Parmesan cheese, thyme, salt, and pepper in a small bowl. After the second round of baking, brush potatoes with this mixture and bake for an additional 30 minutes. Serve.

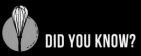 **DID YOU KNOW?**

The Hasselbacken restaurant in Stockholm, Sweden opened its doors in the 18th century and was the first establishment to serve potatoes cut fan-style and then roasted. For best results, avoid floury baking potatoes.

53

GUINEA FOWL WITH LENTILS & LARDONS

SERVES 4

TASTY TIP

Add your favorite blue cheese along with the cream!

DID YOU KNOW?

Often called "the poor man's caviar," Le Puy Green Lentils are the only lentils named after their area of cultivation, and are considered to be the world's best! This revered legume is grown without fertilizer or irrigation, and has a refined taste and firm texture.

Prep time: 30 minutes
Cook time: 1 hour

INGREDIENTS

1 tbsp vegetable oil
1 whole guinea fowl
Salt and freshly ground pepper
1 onion, finely chopped
2 carrots, cut into 1/2-inch cubes
1 cup (250 ml) thick-cut bacon, cut into 1/2-inch pieces (lardons)
2 tbsp olive oil
1 cup (250 ml) Le Puy lentils
1 cup (250 ml) veal stock
1/2 cup (125 ml) 35% cream

PREPARATION

Rub entire surface of guinea fowl with vegetable oil. Season with salt and pepper and place in a roasting pan. Scatter onion, bacon, and carrots around guinea fowl. Pour olive oil over vegetable and bacon mixture and roast in a 350°F (175°C) oven for 30 minutes.

Meanwhile, bring a small pot of water to a boil. Add lentils and let simmer for 20 minutes over low heat. Drain and set aside.

After 30 minutes, baste guinea fowl with its cooking juices. Add lentils to the pan, around the bird. Pour veal stock and cream over the lentil, bacon, and vegetable mixture and mix well to fully incorporate. Raise heat to 400°F (200°C) and cook for another 20 minutes. Carve, or cut into pieces, and serve with lentils, bacon, and vegetables on the side.

54

RED SNAPPER, TOMATOES & FENNEL

SERVES 4

Prep time: 10 minutes
Cook time: 25 minutes

INGREDIENTS

1 whole red snapper, cleaned and scaled
4 sprigs fresh dill
4 Italian tomatoes, halved
1 bulb fennel, cut in half and thinly sliced
1 lemon, cut into 1/4-inch rounds
3 cloves garlic, thinly sliced
1 tbsp sugar
Salt and freshly ground pepper
1/3 cup (80 ml) olive oil

PREPARATION

Brush a baking sheet with a bit of olive oil. Place red snapper in the middle of the baking sheet.

Stuff cavity of red snapper with dill and arrange tomatoes around fish. Top fish with fennel and lemon slices, sprinkle with garlic and sugar, season with salt and pepper, and pour olive oil over all.

Cook in a 400°F (200°C) oven for 20 minutes, and then broil for 3 to 5 minutes, until fennel is lightly golden. Serve.

 **DID YOU KNOW?**

A mature red snapper can weigh up to 50 pounds and live up to 50 years!

55

VEAL, SUNDRIED TOMATOES & GOAT CHEESE

SERVES 8

Prep time: 25 minutes
Cook time: 1 hour and 50 minutes

INGREDIENTS

1 tbsp olive oil
2 cloves garlic, chopped
6 cups baby spinach
1 boneless breast of veal (about 4-1/2 lbs),
trimmed of any excess fat
1 cup (250 ml) store-bought sundried tomato pesto,
or 10 sundried tomatoes, chopped
8 slices prosciutto (about 4-1/2 oz)
7 oz goat cheese
Salt and freshly ground pepper
2 tbsp vegetable oil
2 cups (500 ml) veal stock
2 sprigs fresh rosemary

PREPARATION

In a pan, heat olive oil and sauté garlic for 1 minute. Add spinach and cook for 1 minute, until wilted. Set aside.

Place veal breast on a work surface and brush the side facing up with sundried tomato pesto. Place prosciutto slices vertically and side-by-side on top of the pesto. Spread goat cheese and spinach in a line on top of the prosciutto, about 3 inches from the bottom edge. Roll veal up and around the filling into a tight log. Tie rolled roast up tightly with kitchen string, season with salt and pepper, and pour vegetable oil over all. Place in a roasting pan and pour veal stock around veal. Add rosemary to stock and cook in a 400°F (200°C) oven for 1 hour and 40 minutes, basting veal with its cooking juices every 20 minutes.

After 1 hour and 40 minutes, remove roast from oven, cover with aluminum foil, and let rest for 10 minutes. Slice and serve with cooking juices as a gravy.

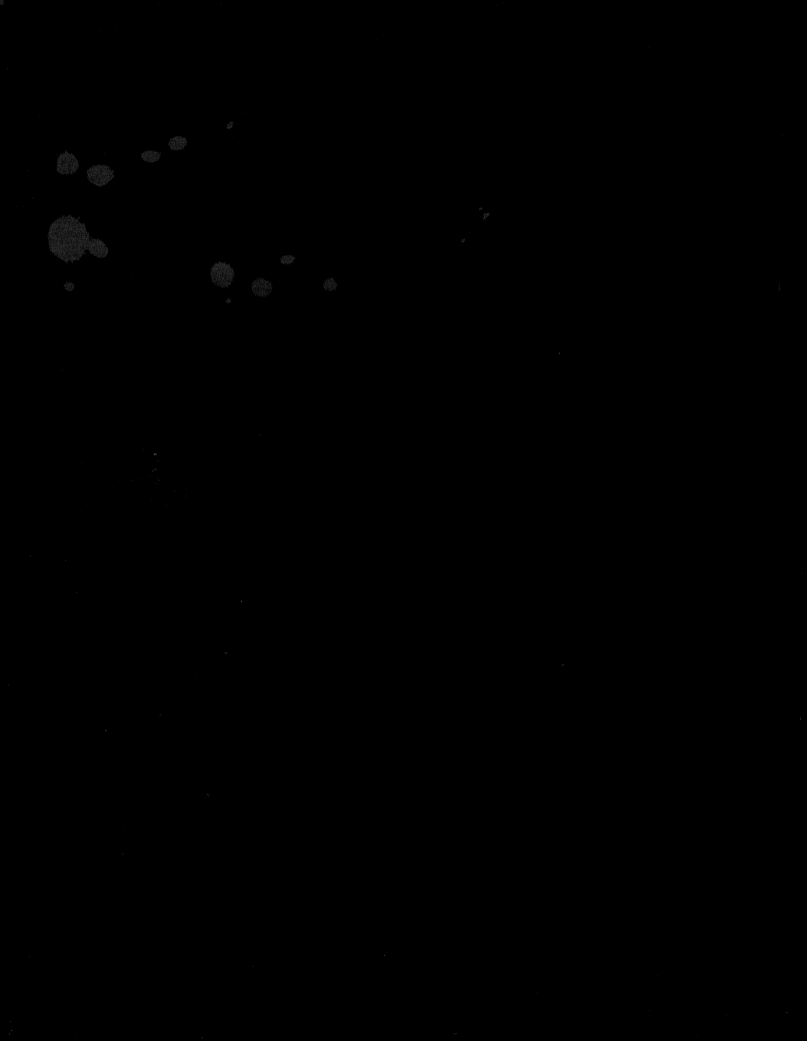

56

RACK OF LAMB WITH POMEGRANATE SAUCE

SERVES 4

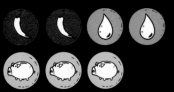

Marinating time: 1 hour
Prep time: 15 minutes
Cook time: 25 minutes

2 racks of lamb
2 tbsp vegetable oil

FOR MAGHREB SEASONING

2 tsp cumin
1 tsp mild paprika
1 tsp ground cardamom
1 tsp brown sugar
1/2 tsp freshly ground pepper
1/4 tsp cayenne pepper
1/2 tsp salt
1 tsp dried oregano
1/2 tsp cinnamon
1 tbsp olive oil

FOR POMEGRANATE SAUCE

2 tbsp honey
1/2 cup (125 ml) water
Juice of 1 fresh pomegranate and a handful of seeds for garnish

PREPARATION

To start, and for a beautiful presentation, use a small knife to trim the excess fat and meat from the exposed bones, scraping in between each bone and removing the sinew and the nerve at the top of each piece.

In a bowl, combine all seasoning ingredients. Rub entire surface of lamb with seasoning and then refrigerate for at least 1 hour.

In a large pan, heat vegetable oil over high heat. Place lamb in the oil, fleshy side down. Use tongs to turn lamb, but only once the bottom is nicely browned.

Pour pomegranate sauce ingredients into a baking dish and mix well. Transfer seared lamb to the the dish, fleshy side up. Roast in a 400°F (200°C) oven for 15 minutes. Let rest for 10 minutes before serving.

57

CRISPY PESTO CHICKEN LEGS

SERVES 4

Marinating time: 4 hours
Prep time: 20 minutes
Cook time: 45 minutes

4 chicken legs

FOR BUTTERMILK MARINADE

1-1/2 cups (375 ml) buttermilk
2 tbsp Dijon mustard
Juice of 1 lemon
1 tsp mild paprika
Salt and freshly ground pepper

FOR TARRAGON PESTO

6 sprigs fresh tarragon
2 cloves garlic
1/4 cup (60 ml) breadcrumbs
2 tbsp Dijon mustard
1/3 cup (80 ml) olive oil

PREPARATION

In a large dish, combine all buttermilk marinade ingredients. Add chicken legs to marinade and toss gently to coat. Cover and refrigerate for at least 4 hours.

In a food processor, combine all tarragon pesto ingredients.

Remove chicken from marinade. Slide a finger under the chicken skin to form a pocket. Spread 1 tbsp pesto evenly between the skin and meat of each chicken leg, and then make sure to securely close each pocket.

Place on a lightly oiled baking sheet and cook in a 350°F (175°C) oven for 45 minutes. Serve.

RISING SUN RIBS

SERVES 4

Marinating time: 12 hours
Prep time: 15 minutes
Cook time: 2 hours

FOR SPARERIBS

2 slabs pork spareribs
8 cups rib brine (see recipe on page 120)

FOR PLUM HOISIN SAUCE

2 plums, pitted and quartered
1 onion
2 cloves garlic
1 inch fresh ginger, peeled
2 fresh chili peppers, halved and seeded
1/4 cup (60 ml) soy sauce
1/4 cup (60 ml) hoisin sauce
Salt and freshly ground pepper

PREPARATION

Place ribs in brine and refrigerate for at least 12 hours.

In a food processor, combine all Asian-style sauce ingredients.

To cook ribs, remove from brine and dry thoroughly. Place on a grill rack in a roasting pan, and pour 1 inch water in the bottom of the pan. Cover and cook in a 300°F (150°C) oven for 1 hour.

After 1 hour, remove cover, brush ribs generously with sauce, and raise oven temperature to 350°F (175°C). Cook ribs for 1 hour longer, brushing with sauce every 30 minutes.

Serve with the side dish of your choice.

TASTY TIP

Use this sauce to make succulent Asian-style chicken wings!

ROASTED CAULIFLOWER

SERVES 4

Prep time: 10 minutes
Cook time: 10 minutes

INGREDIENTS

1 cauliflower, cut into medium florets
2 tbsp sherry vinegar
1/3 cup (80 ml) 35% cream
1/2 cup (125 ml) fresh Parmesan cheese, grated
2 tbsp butter, melted
Salt and freshly ground pepper

PREPARATION

In a bowl, combine all ingredients. Season with salt and pepper and mix well.

Arrange cauliflower on a baking sheet lined with parchment paper. Broil on the center rack for 5 to 10 minutes, or until florets are tender and golden brown. Serve as a side dish.

TASTY TIP

Try this recipe with comté cheese instead of Parmesan.

BEER & MAPLE LAMB

SERVES 4

Prep time: 20 minutes
Cook time: 2 hours and 30 minutes

INGREDIENTS

2 tbsp vegetable oil
4 lamb shanks
Salt and freshly ground pepper
1 onion, finely chopped
2 cloves garlic, chopped
1 bottle (12 oz) dark beer
1 tbsp Dijon mustard
1/4 cup (60 ml) pure maple syrup

PREPARATION

In a large pan, heat oil over high heat and sear lamb shanks, until browned. Season with salt and pepper and transfer to a roasting pan. In the same pan used to sear the lamb, sauté onion and garlic for 2 to 3 minutes. Deglaze pan with beer and pour mixture over lamb shanks. Add Dijon mustard and maple syrup, and mix sauce well.

Cook in a 300°F (150°C) oven for 2 hours and 30 minutes, basting lamb with its cooking juices every 30 minutes. Serve with roasted vegetables.

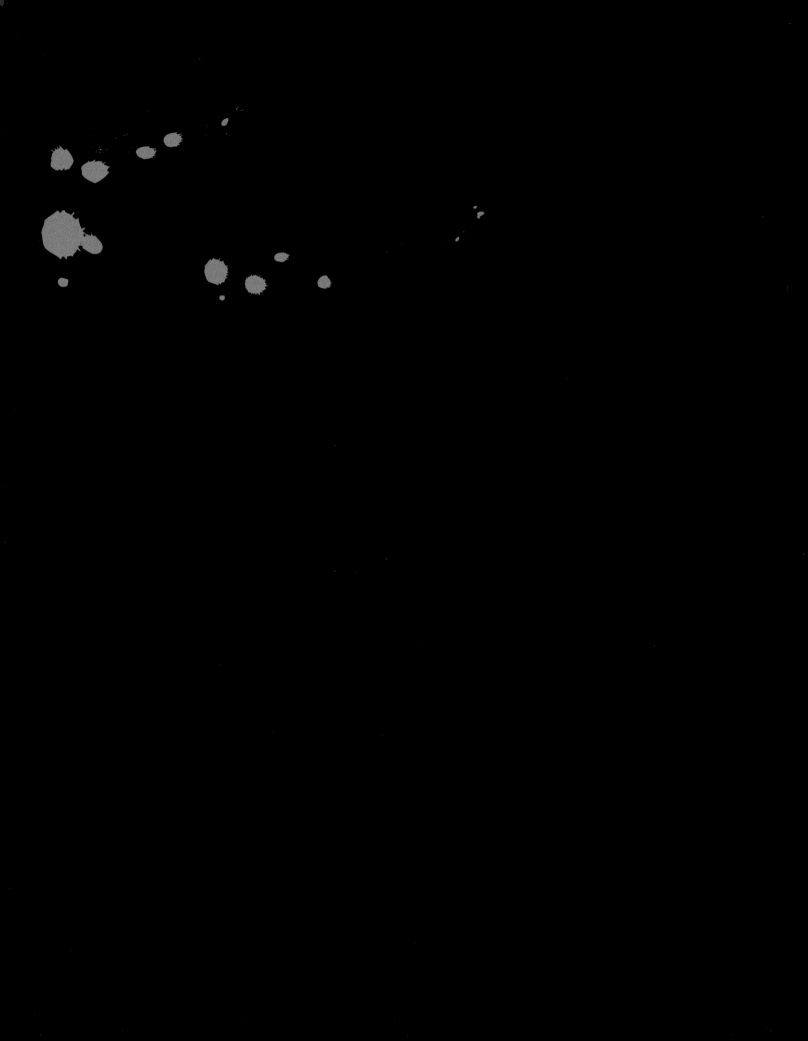

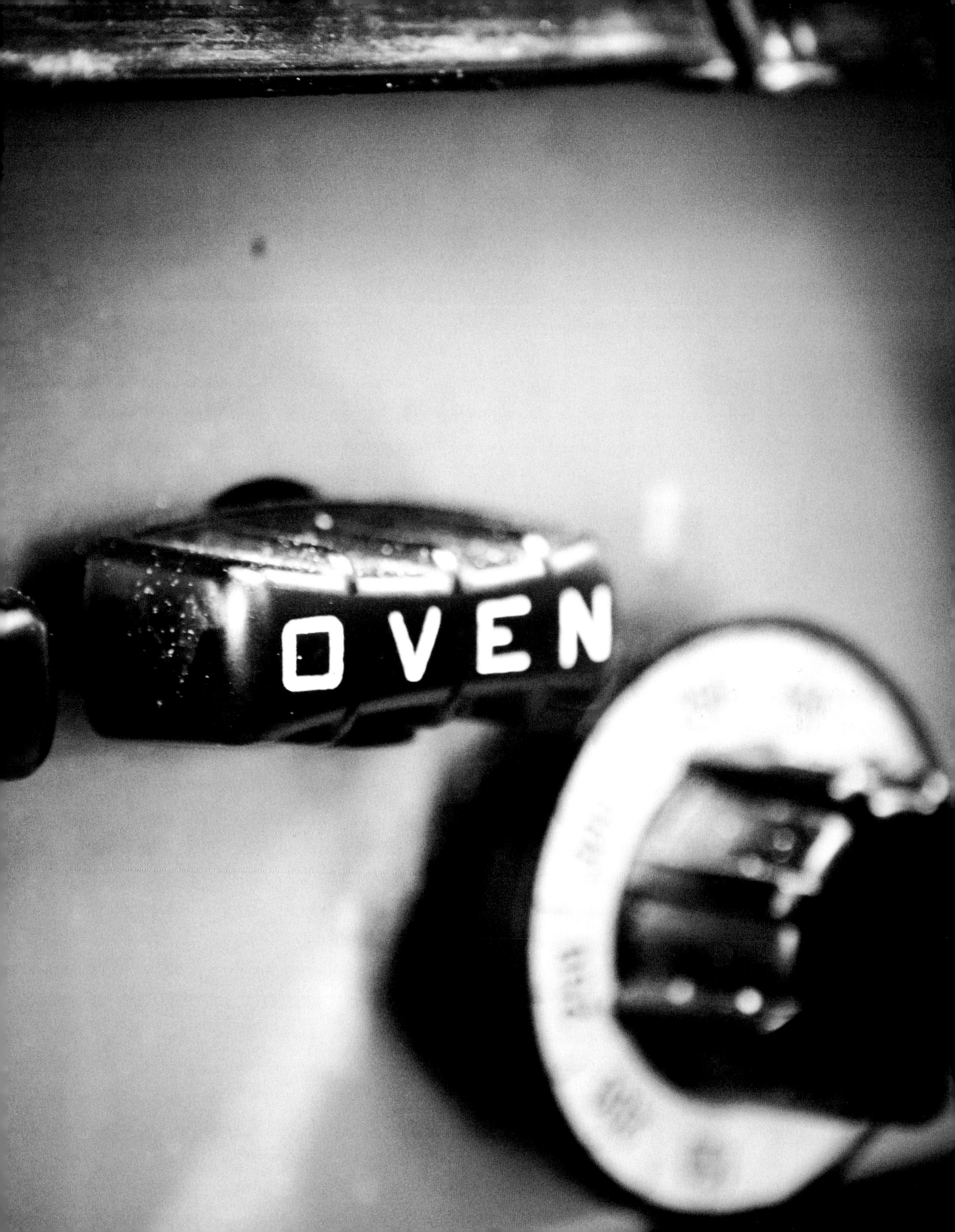
OVEN

INGREDIENTS INDEX

A

ALLSPICE...086
ANCHO CHILI POWDER.....................................040
ANCHOVIES...134
APPLE...058, 148
APPLE JUICE.............................056, 088, 094, 148
ASPARAGUS..062, 096

B

BACON...060, 134, 156
BARBECUE SEASONING.....................................118
BAY LEAVES.........................034, 082, 094, 108, 120
BEEF.................040, 060, 076, 100, 112, 132, 144
BEER, BROWN..094, 172
BEER, PALE ALE..064
BOK CHOY...098
BREAD, BAGUETTE..034
BREAD, CIABATTA...100
BREAD, COUNTRY..048
BREAD, PITA...052
BREADCRUMBS.............................060, 122, 166
BROWN SUGAR....................................032, 040,
...................060, 084, 086, 088, 094, 118, 120, 146, 164
BRUSSELS SPROUTS..056
BUTTERMILK...166
BUTTERNUT SQUASH..128

C

CALVADOS...088
CAPERS..124
CARDAMOM..052, 164
CARROTS............................038, 060, 108, 116, 156
CAULIFLOWER..170

CAYENNE PEPPER 084, 118, 140, 164

CELERY 108

CELERY SALT 118

CHEESE, BLUE 058

CHEESE, GOAT 160

CHEESE, GOUDA 044

CHEESE, LABNEH 052

CHEESE, PARMESAN 104, 122, 154, 170

CHESTNUTS 034

CHICKEN 046, 064, 086, 092, 108, 118, 130, 152, 166

CHICKEN STOCK 050

CHICKPEAS 128

CHILI POWDER 110

CHIVES 056, 076, 100

CILANTRO 106

CINNAMON 050, 052, 152, 164

CLAMS 136

CLOVES 052, 094, 152,

CORIANDER, GROUND 040, 052, 082

CORIANDER SEEDS 108

CORNMEAL 106

CRANBERRY SAUCE 070

CREAM CHEESE 046, 100

CREAM, 35 % 034, 044, 070, 072, 074, 136, 154, 156, 170

CRUSHED RED PEPPER FLAKES 152

CUMIN 052, 148, 164

D

DILL 158

DILL PICKLES 076

DUCK 082

E

EGG 034, 058, 060, 062, 112

EGGPLANT 096

ESPRESSO 040

F

FENNEL 158

FENUGREEK 052

FISH, COD 136

FISH, MONKFISH 124

FISH, RED SNAPPER 158

FISH, SALMON 062, 084

FISH, TROUT 106

G

GARLIC 032, 034, 036, 038, 048, 052, 058, 060,
..... 062, 064, 082, 086, 092, 096, 104, 108, 120, 122, 124, 128,
.... 134, 168, 142, 144, 146, 152, 158, 160, 166, 168, 172

GARLIC POWDER 040, 084, 110, 118

GINGER 052, 082, 152, 168

GRAPEVINE LEAVES 036

GUINEA FOWL 156

H

HAM 094

HONEY 046, 050, 082, 094, 116, 128, 164

HORSERADISH 076

K

KETCHUP 120, 130

L

LAMB 036, 052, 122, 146, 164, 172
LEMON 036, 052,
.... 064, 092, 096, 106, 124, 128, 140, 146, 152, 158, 166
LENTILS 156
LETTUCE 100
LIQUID SMOKE 110, 120

M

MACE 086
MANGO 106, 152
MAPLE SYRUP 088, 172,
MARROW BONES 048
MILD PAPRIKA 034, 052, 084, 108, 110, 118, 140, 164, 166
MINT 036, 052
MIRIN 098
MOLASSES 120
MUSHROOMS, BUTTON 034, 060, 068, 092
MUSHROOMS, PORTOBELLO 074, 100
MUSHROOMS, WILD 092
MUSTARD SEEDS 108
MUSTARD, DIJON 088, 122, 132, 134, 146, 166, 172
MUSTARD, DRY 084, 110, 118, 142
MUSTARD, WHOLEGRAIN 044, 100

N

NUTMEG 052, 086
NUTS, PECANS 148

O

OLIVES, BLACK 146
OLIVES, KALAMATA 072, 124
ONION 032,
...... 038, 052, 060, 064, 108, 118, 120, 132, 144, 156, 168, 172
ONION POWDER 040, 084, 118

ONION, GREEN

ONION, GREEN 086, 134
ONION, RED 046, 068, 070, 096
ORANGE 082
ORANGE MARMELADE 084
OREGANO 036, 072, 080, 096, 140, 164

P

PARSLEY 068, 080, 104, 122, 148
PEACH 050
PEPPER, BELL 068, 080, 096
PEPPER, CHILI 168
PEPPER, HABANERO 086
PICKLED BEETS 076
PLAIN YOGURT 152
PLUM 168
POMEGRANATE 164
PORK 032, 044, 050, 058, 074, 088, 110, 120, 142, 168
PORT 070
POTATO 032, 038, 088, 108, 140, 142, 154
PROSCIUTTO 044, 058, 124, 160
PUFF PASTRY 058

Q

QUAIL 098

R

RABBIT 134
RED GRAPES 046
ROSEMARY 034, 038, 144, 146, 160

S

SAGE 044, 070
SAKE 098
SAUCE, CHILI 032, 106

SAUCE, HARISSA...052
SAUCE, HOISIN..168
SAUCE, HOT...130
SAUCE, PIRI-PIRI...064
SAUCE, SOY................032, 076, 082, 088, 098, 168
SAUCE, TABASCO...120, 124
SAUCE, WORCESTERSHIRE..............................120, 132
SAUSAGE...034, 068
SAUSAGE, CHORIZO..032
SEA SALT...048
SESAME SEEDS...098
SHALLOT.................072, 074, 076, 112, 136
SORREL...136
SOUR CREAM...076
SPINACH..160
STAR ANISE...050
STEAK SPICE...112, 130
SUMAC..052
SUNDRIED TOMATO PESTO..160
SWEET POTATO...038, 148

T

TAHINI...128
TANDOORI SPICE...152
TARRAGON...112, 166
THYME..032, 034,
.......038, 048, 074, 082, 086, 092, 108, 110, 120, 122, 132, 154
TOMATO...................032, 052, 096, 100, 106, 158
TOMATOES, CHERRY...072
TOMATOES, CRUSHED (CANNED)...................................060
TOMATOES, SUNDRIED.....................................134, 160
TOMATO PASTE...120
TURKEY...034, 070
TURNIP...038

V

VEAL...072, 160
VEAL STOCK..070, 156, 160
VINEGAR, APPLE CIDER...............032, 088, 116, 148
VINEGAR, BALSAMIC.................................050, 068, 096
VINEGAR, RED WINE.................................070, 106, 120, 144
VINEGAR, RICE..082
VINEGAR, SHERRY...................046, 074, 080, 134, 170
VINEGAR, WHITE...130, 152
VINEGAR, WHITE WINE..112

W

WALNUTS..056
WHISKY...120
WINE, RED...040, 132, 144
WINE, WHITE.........032, 036, 044, 072, 074, 112, 134, 136, 146

Z

ZA'ATAR..128
ZUCCHINI...096

MARINADES, GLAZES, SAUCES, SEASONINGS, ETC.

BARBECUE RUB 084

BRINE, CHICKEN 108

BRINE, DUCK 082

BRINE, RIBS 120

BRINE, TURKEY 034

CLASSIC VINAIGRETTE 080

GLAZE, BARBECUE 032

GLAZE, CRANBERRY 070

GLAZE, MAPLE CALVADOS 088

GLAZE, PEKING 082

HUMMUS 128

MANGO CHUTNEY 152

MANGO SALSA 106

MARINADE, BUTTERMILK 166

MARINADE, JERK 086

MARINADE, PIRI-PIRI 064

MARINADE, RED WINE 144

MARINADE, SAKE 098

MARINADE, SPICY 130

MARINADE, SUNDRIED TOMATO 134

MARINADE, TANDOORI 152

MARINADE, WHITE WINE 036

OLIVE TAPENADE 124

PERSILLADE 122

SALT CRUST 062

SAUCE, BARBECUE WHISKY 120

SAUCE, BÉARNAISE 112

SAUCE, CLAM 136

SAUCE, PLUM HOISIN 168

SAUCE, POMEGRANATE 164

SEASONING, ANCHO ESPRESSO 040

SEASONING, MAGHREB 164

SEASONING, SHAWARMA 052

SEASONING, SMOKY 110

TARRAGON PESTO 166

CONVERSION CHART

1 dl .... 10 cl......................... 100 ml
1 tablespoon .... 15 ml
1 teaspoon .... 5 ml
1 oz.. 30 ml
1 cup... 250 ml
4 cups ....1 l
1/2 cup.. 125 ml
1/4 cup... 60 ml
1/3 cup... 80 ml
1 lb .... 450 g
2 lbs .... 900 g
2.2 lbs ....1 kg
400°F.................. 200°C T/7
350°F................. 175°C T/6
300°F................. 150°C T/5

Volume Conversion
* Approximate values

---

1 cup (250 ml) crumbled cheese .... 150 g
1 cup (250 ml) all-purpose flour.................. 115 g
1 cup (250 ml) white sugar........................ 200 g
1 cup (250 ml) brown sugar .... 220 g
1 cup (250 ml) butter .... 230 g
1 cup (250 ml) oil................................... 215 g
1 cup (250 ml) canned tomatoes................ 250 g

NOTES

60

IN THE SAME COLLECTION

THE WORLD'S 60 BEST
SALADS
PERIOD.

THE WORLD'S 60 BEST
PASTA SAUCES
PERIOD.

THE WORLD'S 60 BEST
BURGERS
PERIOD.

THE WORLD'S 60 BEST
LUNCHES
PERIOD.

THE WORLD'S 60 BEST
RECIPES FOR STUDENTS
PERIOD.

THE WORLD'S 60 BEST
PIZZAS
PERIOD.

THE WORLD'S 60 BEST
GRATINS
PERIOD.

THE WORLD'S 60 BEST
STUFFED DISHES
PERIOD.

THE WORLD'S **60** BEST
HEALTHY SMOOTHIES
PERIOD.

THE WORLD'S **60** BEST
SOUPS
PERIOD.

THE WORLD'S **60** BEST
STEWS
PERIOD.

THE WORLD'S **60** BEST
DESSERTS
PERIOD.